PASTOR AARON CRABB

NEXT

WITH AMANDA CRABB

EMBRACE YOUR PROMOTION AND UNLOCK THE NEW LEVEL

FOREWORD BY DR. ROD PARSLEY

I am blessed to call Aaron and Amanda Crabb my friends. They are dynamic leaders in the body of Christ, with a message of faith, power, and redemption. This book shares their journey and the powerful principles they used to overcome and break free from every demonic attack. It will stir your faith and equip you to do exploits in the kingdom of God.

Ryan LeStrange, Author
Atlanta, Georgia
Hell's Toxic Trio

What a team these two are! I love the way they flow in life and ministry together. This book is a game changer. One ounce of obedience will do more for you than all the prayer in the world. *NEXT* has the answers to the questions you've been asking. It's going to set your heart ablaze and prepare you for your NEXT!

Real Talk Kim, Pastor and Author
Limitless Church
Fayetteville, Georgia
Shut Hell Up

From the moment I first met Pastors Aaron and Amanda, it was obvious they were living for their NEXT! It was evident where they had been with God, which produced a confidence that whatever was NEXT in their lives would not only be with God but also for the glory of God. In reading this book, you will be inspired, encouraged, and want to live for your NEXT.

Greg DeVries, Pastor and Author
The Well
Scottsboro, Alabama
Taking It to the Streets

Have you ever felt that where you are is not where God intended for you to stay, but where He is taking you seems so much bigger than you, your resources, your experiences, or your knowledge? NEXT is the "next" book you need in your life—RIGHT NOW!! Pastors Aaron and Amanda Crabb, shepherds with the heart of God (you couldn't ask for better), release timeless biblical truths that they have personally walked through, showing us how the Holy Spirit helps us navigate from where we are to where God wants us to be. If you're reading this right now, don't stop reading because you're NEXT!!

Eddie James
Eddie James Ministries
Ocoee, Tennessee

Aaron and Amanda Crabb have been our guests on "LIFE Today." They also sang at our Christmas banquet a few years ago. A short time after that, they stepped out of their comfort zone and embraced God's NEXT for their lives: planting a church in Tennessee. Through these pages, the Crabbs will encourage you to recognize that your NEXT is ahead. If you've ever missed the mark and think your life is over, there is a kingdom opportunity ahead. You'll be inspired by the biblical and personal stories they share—all pointing to the fact that you don't have to remain stuck in the wilderness. God's NEXT is always filled with promise and kingdom purpose—trust Him for the NEXT steps He has prepared for you!

James Robison
LIFE Outreach International
Fort Worth, Texas

Next:
Embrace Your Promotion and Unlock the Next Level

CONTENTS

FOREWORD

I am proud to have the privilege of calling Aaron and Amanda Crabb my spiritual son and daughter in the faith. They are not afraid to hold on to the values that have served past generations well, but they refuse to be satisfied with the victories of days gone by.

They are relentlessly optimistic, forward-thinking and faith-oriented individuals. They represent the very best of their generation—innovative, creative, collaborative, and anointed to proclaim truth in music, preaching, writing and other avenues yet to be explored.

They consistently reject the enemy's enticements to become mired in the flatlands of shallow spiritual existence. They are continually seeking the sunlit uplands of new experiences, new horizons, and new victories for the kingdom of God.

Their book, *NEXT*, will encourage you, inspire you and challenge you to allow God to do everything through you He wants to do, so that you can become all He wants you to be. Your NEXT is in your future—not in your past. Hear God's voice, follow His leading, and discover your NEXT!

Dr. Rod Parsley, Pastor
World Harvest Church
Columbus, Ohio

ACKNOWLEDGMENTS

It is with great excitement that Amanda and I release this book into your hands. First and foremost, we want to thank our Lord and Savior Jesus Christ for saving us, changing us, and filling us with the power of His Holy Spirit.

Amanda and I especially want to thank our families for their continual love and support in everything we do.

We are thankful for the amazing people we pastor at Restoring Hope Church. You provide an incredible environment for us to preach and proclaim the best news in all the world. We are humbled that you would allow us to be a voice in your lives.

We also want to thank those whose editing and graphics abilities helped make this book possible. Your gifts and talents have contributed to the completion of this work. Thank you for seeing this book through!

Last, but not least, thank you to our four amazing children! Elijah, Eva, Ean, and Eda: you are the reason and the motivation for everything we do. We know that every NEXT you experience will be above and beyond anything that we could ask, think or imagine. We love you!

Pastors Aaron and Amanda Crabb
Restoring Hope Church
Hendersonville, Tennessee

INTRODUCTION:

OUT OF THE DARKNESS, INTO THE LIGHT

In the beginning God created the heavens and the earth. The earth was without form, and void; and darkness was on the face of the deep. And the Spirit of God was hovering over the face of the waters.

Then God said, "Let there be light;" and there was light. And God saw the light, that it was good; and God divided the light from the darkness. God called the light Day, and the darkness He called Night. So the evening and the morning were the first day.

Genesis 1:1-5

FROM THE DESK OF AARON:

The lights on the life flight helicopter flashed as it rose into the air. Onboard were two tiny twin babies who had been born too soon, and whose lives were hanging in the balance. My brother Adam and I had been born prematurely. As a result, our lungs were not fully developed.

Our mother was left behind as we were transported to a hospital in a neighboring city, which had the equipment necessary to keep us alive. She had not even been able to hold us in her arms before the emergency team whisked us away.

Machines regulated our breathing. Heat lamps kept our bodies at the correct temperature. An intertwining assortment of wires and tubes crisscrossed our incubators.

At birth, Adam weighed 4 pounds, 7 ounces; I weighed 4 pounds, 3 ounces. We both went down to under 3 pounds before things started to turn for the better. We remained hospitalized until we were strong enough to breathe on our own and had gained sufficient weight. It was a dark time, a precarious beginning.

Creation has a beginning and an end. God's Word declares that He is the first and the last, the Alpha and the Omega. Creation was initiated from a place of darkness; our lives began in a time of darkness.

Clearly the enemy's plan began early in my life, but the story doesn't end there. My life has been filled with stories of uphill-climbing moments and low-valley experiences. Each story has led me and my wife, Amanda, toward our divine purpose and into the will of God for our lives.

If we have lived life at all, we understand that there are many beginnings, endings and transitions, and it is in those transitional moments that we are stretched and pulled. It can be very difficult, but very necessary in order for us to advance into the NEXT season God has for us.

God moved upon our hearts to write this book and to declare the word NEXT as our theme. A NEXT is a time or season coming which immediately follows the present.

A NEXT also follows in a specific order. God's way of movement is forward. While we might find ourselves at a complete halt, there is always a NEXT upcoming.

As Amanda and I share with you some biblical truths and some personal moments of NEXT, our prayer is that you will have the courage and strength to believe that no matter what your current situation may look like or where you may be in life, God always has a NEXT in place for you. Your NEXT is more than you could think, ask or imagine. Follow us as we travel through some pivotal places—some seasons of hardship—that led us through new chapters and into new territory.

Aaron Crabb, Pastor
Restoring Hope Church
Hendersonville, Tennessee

Chapter One

THE DESTINY OF A DREAMER

And Reuben said to them, "Shed no blood, but cast him into this pit which is in the wilderness, and do not lay a hand on him"—that he might deliver him out of their hands, and bring him back to his father. So it came to pass, when Joseph had come to his brothers, that they stripped Joseph of his tunic, the tunic of many colors that was on him. Then they took him and cast him into a pit. And the pit was empty; there was no water in it.

Genesis 37:22-24

And Pharaoh said to Joseph, "See, I have set you over all the land of Egypt." Then Pharaoh took his signet ring off his hand and put it on Joseph's hand; and he clothed him in garments of fine linen and put a gold chain around his neck. And he had him ride in the second chariot which he had; and they cried out before him, "Bow the knee!" So he set him over all the land of Egypt. Pharaoh also said to Joseph, "I am Pharaoh, and without your consent no man may lift his hand or foot in all the land of Egypt."

Genesis 41:41-44

NEXT

FROM THE DESK OF AARON:

One Sunday afternoon when I was just a young boy, I was taking a nap at my grandmother's house, and I begin to dream about the church my father pastored. In the dream, I walked into the sanctuary and saw lanterns and candles scattered around the room.

This scene reminded me of the old-fashioned services we would have from time to time. I sat down in the third row, and something caught my eye. I saw a demonic figure standing in the pulpit, staring back at me. This figure spoke up and said, "I'm going to destroy everything!"

Suddenly, I woke up. As I opened my eyes—trying to focus—I saw that the demonic apparition from my dream was now standing at the foot of the bed. His presence was terrifying; his eyes were pure evil. Fear and intimidation paralyzed me.

I opened my mouth to speak, but no sound came out. I tried again—nothing. On my third attempt, my voice returned, and I was able to say, "Jesus!" His presence immediately filled the room and the demonic force instantly disappeared.

My grandmother, who had witnessed all this, began praying and pleading the blood of Jesus over me. I truly believe that this spirit was trying to attach itself to my life and destroy my purpose. For many years, fear and intimidation had a tight grasp on me. Satan wanted to destroy my future ministry because he knew the magnitude of its potential effects.

THROWN INTO THE PIT

Even a casual reading of the Bible gives us stories of men and women who were called and anointed by God for a specific purpose yet were thwarted on every side before their dreams came to pass. Joseph was one such man.

Joseph was anointed, highly favored by God and by his earthly father. Although God gave him a destiny and placed a dream in his heart, the fulfillment of that dream did not come without challenge or without cost.

Joseph was hated by his brothers. He was betrayed, rejected, stripped of his coat of many colors, thrown into a pit, and left for dead. I can only imagine the anguish he suffered. It was not until much later that he would find that both his dream and his destiny were greater than his circumstances.

The same God who placed that dream inside Joseph is still placing dreams in people's hearts today. It often begins as a thread that is interwoven throughout a person's life, until it is later perceived, understood and acted upon.

At an early age, God gave me a passion to be in His presence. His glory had such a magnetic power to it, and I was deeply drawn to Him. Many times, I saw Jesus saving, healing, delivering and transforming lives.

I grew up in the city of Beaver Dam, in a rural area of western Kentucky, where my father was a Pentecostal preacher in a local church.

Because of the sometimes-exhausting nature of church work, many "preacher's kids" or "PK's" as they are called, run from ministry life. In our church, pews would many nights serve as beds for sleepy children when services ran long. Our family time would be put on hold as the needs of the people in our congregation were put first. We lived on limited means and felt the pressure of living under a microscope.

But God had placed a longing in me. He protected and defended my heart as I was growing up, and I wanted nothing more than to be close to Him. I loved being in His presence.

When it was time for another camp meeting, I could not contain my excitement; I had such a great expectation and anticipation for more of Him. The response of the people toward God in these services always fascinated me. I loved to watch the way they passionately worshiped and praised God. I could tell that God's Word was life to them. Although I did not fully comprehend all that was taking place, it fostered within me the desire for more of God.

Back at home in my bedroom, I would reenact what I had experienced at the camp meeting by singing, preaching, and forming my own prayer lines.

I remember one particular night of revival when I was nine years old. A woman named Dolly came for prayer. She appeared lifeless and full of gloom and doom, with no evidence of joy. All that changed when Dolly had her own personal encounter with the Holy Ghost. As she was prayed for, the Spirit of God fell on her, and she broke out in irrepressible laughter. She received a breakthrough and was completely transformed. From that night forward and every time the Holy Ghost moved through the congregation, Dolly would break out in laughter under the power of God, and the spiritual chains would begin to fall from everyone around her. She became consumed with joy.

For years, I didn't even know her real name was *Dolly*. In my mind, her name was *Joy* and it was unspeakable and full of glory! She was free, and it reminded me of the scripture: *"Now the Lord is the Spirit; and where the Spirit of the Lord is, there is liberty"* (2 Corinthians 3:17).

But my personal joy would soon be challenged for the first time when life took an unexpected turn: my parents filed for divorce. The stable home life I knew crumbled. Fear began to take hold of me. Insecurity and discouragement came in like a flood. As a result, I became so shy that I could barely look at anyone, let alone speak to people. The desire for God was still there, but I found myself thrown into a pit—just like Joseph in Genesis 41.

My parents' divorce was painful. Our once secure and solid home had been shattered. Peace and comfort in the home became a distant memory.

Many nights, I would see my mom lying on the floor of our home in tears, praying that God would fix things and that her family would be restored. Our home life was a mess and no longer picture perfect. Broken promises, broken hearts, and broken dreams had replaced a home full of love. The enemy felt he had won; but with God, there is always a NEXT. There is always a purpose that comes from the pain. *"Weeping may endure for a night, but joy comes in the morning"* (Psalm 30:5).

NEXT

There may be those of you reading this book who feel like you are in a bad chapter of your life. You might be discouraged and feel like your dream has died, but don't misunderstand where you are in your situation. There is always a *mess* before the *message* and there is always a *trial* before the *triumph*. There is always a *devastation* before the *restoration*. What is broken now will be restored for a greater purpose.

> Trial
> Before
> Triumph

At nine years old, I could have never imagined what God had in store for my NEXT. God put many of the broken pieces back together by applying His blood and making something beautiful out of them, as the Word of God says in Romans 8:28: *"And we know that all things work together for good to those who love God, to those who are the called according to His purpose."*

In 1994, my father, Gerald, and his wife, Kathy Crabb Hannah, put together—by the leading of the Holy Spirit—a small singing group known as The Crabb Family.

The Crabb Family was a fusion of five siblings who had no idea where God was about to lead them and the doors of opportunity He was about to open for them.

As God led us through a whirlwind of success, we achieved many number one Gospel Music songs and awards. The Crabb Family sang and toured together from 1994 to 2007. During that time, we saw many souls coming to know Christ. We were featured on many different musical stages and many television networks and radio stations. We became internationally known and experienced a global outreach.

TURNING THE PAGE

In 2007, though, the Crabb Family disbanded, and we all began pursuing our own music ministry careers. My wife, Amanda, and I formed our own contemporary Christian music duo. We created several albums and began traveling and ministering together—which we still do. We also served for a period of time as worship leaders at Cornerstone Church in San Antonio, Texas.

During the season that I toured with the Crabb family, the one constant in my life was the powerful connection I felt to the lyrics and melodies that impacted people around the world. I'm reminded of Paul's words in 1 Thessalonians 5:16-18: *"Rejoice always, pray without ceasing, in everything give thanks; for this is the will of God in Christ Jesus for you."*

I remember the day I told my classmates I was going to travel around sharing the Gospel of Jesus through my music. Most looked back at me like I had lost my mind. The principal agreed with their reactions and said, "You will never amount to anything."

Joseph was misunderstood, wrongly treated, and thrown into a dark pit all because he had a dream. In the same way, I was ridiculed and misunderstood because I had a dream to share the gospel with my music. I had a dream to share my passion for the Lord. Jeremiah 29:11 says, *"'For I know the thoughts that I think toward you,' says the LORD, 'thoughts of peace and not of evil, to give you a future and a hope.'"* God's Word is true and speaks to your destiny, but those who are not led by the Spirit will not understand.

Just like Joseph's dream, my dream was tested—yours will be tested, too. Your passion and desire must be the fuel that keeps you going. Even when Joseph was lied about, rejected, betrayed, and thrown into a pit, his passion and desire produced power for him to move into his NEXT. He never stopped dreaming, and he never stopped being faithful to the Lord.

There have been times when the words of others, or even words of my own have pushed me in a dark place of defeat and despair, but I held on. I held onto my dream, my place of promise.

You can, too. You are about to disappoint those enemies who pushed you into the pit. You are about to disrupt all their plans. You will not die there; God has a plan to prosper you and to give you hope and a future, just as it says in Jeremiah 29:11.

I encourage you to let your passion for your dream keep pushing you forward even when you don't feel like it. Look at the life of Jesus. Sometimes, passion will pull you into problems, but those problems are a *set up* for your *get up*.

The greatest display of power followed the passion of our Lord and Savior Jesus Christ. As Christ humbled himself through His death and the crucifixion on the cross, it released the resurrection power of Almighty God. I want to encourage you that there is no gladness without sadness, there is no healing without sickness, and there is no resurrection without the crucifixion.

> Resurrection Power

When you come to the end of a chapter in your life, simply turn the page. Some chapters of your life may have been difficult. You may have experienced things that you didn't deserve and that you couldn't change.

You may have done things that you knew were wrong. You may have let anger and resentment, or hatred and unforgiveness fill your heart, but that was the last chapter and now it is time to read on. In your last chapter, you might have been broken, humiliated, miserable, lame, angry, hurting, or even disappointed. In the last chapter, you may have experienced loneliness and cried many tears, but that was *then*, and this is NEXT.

Don't judge your story based on a painful chapter. The last chapter may have been terrible, but your life doesn't end there. All the chapters of a book have one thing in common: they come to an end. That does not mean your life is over. It simply means that one chapter must end so another can begin. It means that there is more to the story, and the best is truly yet to come.

Look how the story played out for Joseph. Joseph was initially cast into a pit by his jealous brothers. He was then sold as a slave and eventually thrown into jail. During his time in jail—because he could interpret dreams—he found favor with Pharaoh who promoted him to chief officer of the land. God had a NEXT in mind all along.

Consider your own situation as it relates to Joseph. Have you been betrayed by someone close to you? Have their actions pushed you into a pit? Like Joseph, you may have been stripped of your coat of many colors. You may have lost your job, or you may have gone through a painful divorce. The enemy may be after your house, your health, or your peace, but consider Joseph: his latter end was far greater than his humble beginning.

The devil always tries to kill the dreamer, but today's attacked dreamer is tomorrow's promised deliverer. The enemy may be trying to kill your dream, but the place of NEXT is a place of deliverance. The Bible says that Joseph dreamed again and produced many dreams. I encourage you to dream again.

Does it feel like the enemy is closing in on you, and God is a million miles away? You can sympathize with the man at the pool of Bethesda who suffered for 38 long years. I don't know how long the season you are facing has lasted or will last, but I know that with God, there is always a NEXT, where all things will be made new. I can assure you that a new dimension, a fresh anointing—your NEXT—is coming!

DECLARATIONS FOR A DREAMER

Here is my prayer for you and my declaration over your future. You can take my words and make them your words and use them to propel yourself into your NEXT:

- *I pray that desire will manifest now as an unrelenting, undying drive that will move you forward.*

- *I pray that your passion will push you toward your purpose.*

- *I declare that no matter what the moment looks and feels like, it is making room for what is about to happen.*

- *I declare that you will see miracles, signs, and wonders.*

- *I renounce fear, disappointment, and disillusionment in Jesus' name.*

- *I speak to the spirit man inside of you: "Refuse to quit!"*

- *I declare the word NEXT over you. A new chapter is coming!*

- *I declare that you will not give up, because you will come out of this place of darkness, disappointment, or depression and step into your NEXT, your place of destiny and purpose.*

- *I declare that you will hold on to your dream and keep believing because your NEXT is about to happen!*

Chapter Two

STRANGE THINGS

Now it happened on a certain day, as He was teaching, that there were Pharisees and teachers of the law sitting by, who had come out of every town of Galilee, Judea, and Jerusalem. And the power of the Lord was present to heal them. Then behold, men brought on a bed a man who was paralyzed, whom they sought to bring in and lay before Him.

And when they could not find how they might bring him in, because of the crowd, they went up on the housetop and let him down with his bed through the tiling into the midst before Jesus.

When He saw their faith, He said to him, "Man, your sins are forgiven you."

And the scribes and the Pharisees began to reason, saying, "Who is this who speaks blasphemies? Who can forgive sins but God alone?"

But when Jesus perceived their thoughts, He answered and said to them, "Why are you reasoning in your hearts? Which is easier, to say, 'Your sins are forgiven you,' or to say, 'Rise up and walk'? But that you may know that the Son of Man has power on earth to forgive sins" — He said to the man who was paralyzed, "I say to you, arise, take up your bed, and go to your house."

Immediately he rose up before them, took up what he had been lying on, and departed to his own house, glorifying God. And they were all amazed, and they glorified God and were filled with fear, saying, "We have seen strange things today!"

Luke 5:17-26

FROM THE DESK OF AMANDA:

T he church Aaron and I pastor, Restoring Hope Church, called for a three-week corporate fast in July 2017. We prayed, fasted, and sought God's face for 21 days in preparation for our miracle prayer service, which kicked off a special meeting we were holding called Overflow 2017. We were serious about our desire to experience the power and presence of God.

On the day the fast ended, we anticipated an atmosphere of power and authority. We were expecting to see extraordinary things that night during our prayer service, and indeed, we did. The presence of God was thick, heavy, and intense. We could see the glory cloud hovering over us as it draped across the sanctuary.

Aaron and I formed an old-fashioned prayer tunnel, along with members of our prayer team. The line of people waiting for prayer extended around the perimeter of the sanctuary and filled up the rows. We had not expected that many people to show up.

As people began to walk through the tunnel, they described it as electrifying. Many people experienced healing within the tunnel—before they even received direct prayer from us. The changes were unbelievable. We saw blind eyes opened, deaf ears unlocked, tumors reduced, addictions broken, and marriages restored. That night, many received the NEXT in their walk with God. It was an inexplicable encounter, to say the least.

UNFAMILIAR TERRITORY

"We have seen STRANGE things today!"

If you have ever left a church service and heard this or said this, you probably wouldn't want to go back for more—unless you were the one that the strangeness affected.

A strange thing is something that is unusual or surprising, something unsettling or hard to understand—something out of the ordinary.

Truthfully, many of us are terrified that something strange might happen in church, and it might make our friends uncomfortable. For instance, we invite that one person to church and then pray that the Holy Ghost doesn't show up and show out. We pray, "Lord, please don't let Sister Martha spin around in the spirit like a tornado" or "Please don't let Brother Harris give a tongue and interpretation."

But where Jesus traveled, strange things followed: healing, deliverance, miracles.

Hebrews 11:1 says, *"Now faith is the substance of things hoped for, the evidence of things not seen."* To move in faith, we must stop looking with our natural eyes. We don't move mountains with our eyes; we move them with our faith.

NEXT

News of Jesus and His healing power had traveled throughout Galilee, Judea and Jerusalem. This man's friends may have heard about the way Jesus responded to the leper who asked Him if He was willing to heal him: "*I am willing; be cleansed*" (Luke 5:13). They believed that if they could get their friend to Jesus, He would have that same compassion on him and heal him, too. They believed there was a NEXT for him.

These friends were desperate—so desperate that when they couldn't find a way through the crowd of people, they climbed up on the housetop and lowered their friend down through the ceiling right into the midst of the crowd around Jesus.

Not too many of us could say that we would go to this extreme to help a friend in need. Many of us believe in the power of God to heal, but how many of us will put in the work to see it through?

We have all experienced being in an uncomfortable place. Declare this over your life: *Today is a totally different day. Desperate times call for desperate measures.*

We have learned that God doesn't often use the comfortable places in our life to reveal His power to us. Sometimes we must tread into unfamiliar territory to find a miracle, and we must allow ourselves to see and experience strange things.

Isaiah 43:19 says, "*Behold, I will do a new thing, Now it shall spring forth; Shall you not know it? I will even make a road in the wilderness and rivers in the desert.*" What Isaiah is saying in this text is that there is a NEXT for us.

Too often, we are more worried about attending the popular gathering that has the biggest building or that preaches a well-crafted inspirational message. However, the Word of God is inspiring all by itself! God is ready for His church to rise up, to expect the unexpected, and to have faith that He will do what He said He would do.

The man whose friends let him down through the ceiling couldn't get to Jesus on his own. We all have those friends who can't quite get it together. They are in need, and they need us to be desperate for them. Although they can't see it themselves, their breakthrough might just be contingent on us carrying them to Jesus!

We say things like, "Well, they've been in that situation for years. There isn't really anything I could do for them at this point." But we must be willing to bring them to Jesus, even if it means we have to find creative ways to get them there.

We don't know this man's backstory. We don't know why he was paralyzed or why his friends were carrying him. Did they lower him through the roof out of love for him, or were they just tired of carrying him around? Again, we don't know the *why*; all we know for sure is that they were determined to get him to Jesus.

Perhaps you are carrying around a painful past, or the weight of a difficult situation with a child, a spouse, a family member, or even a co-worker. You may be wondering how you are going to carry them to Jesus, when many of them won't even step foot into a meeting or a service where they might meet Him.

NEXT

When you are carrying significant issues like this around, there is often more to them than meets the eye. The plan of God goes far beyond what we can see with the natural eye, hear with the natural ear, or perceive with the natural senses. We see in part, but God sees the big picture. He will prompt us to pray, so that He can move in our lives to accomplish His will and His purpose. Although we may feel that the burden of someone's need is too heavy for us to carry, God will always make a way to bring His plan to pass.

CARRYING MY SECOND CHILD

One night, Aaron came out from his prayer time with the Lord and said, "We are going to have a little girl! I saw her—she was about 10 or 11 years old and had long blonde hair."

I was shocked because we hadn't even talked about having a second child at that time. All I could say was, "Really?"

Some time later, when we found out we were expecting, we were beyond excited. We knew this was the little girl that Aaron had seen in the vision. We began to pray over her as our daughter, even before her gender was confirmed. Aaron had already seen her, and we knew it would come to pass.

One day in my prayer closet, I was praying over her and speaking things into existence in her life. We had a name already picked out, so as I was praying, I called her by her planned name. I plainly heard the Holy Spirit speak these exact words to me: "You shall name this child *Eva*, because her name will mean *life*. There will be days the enemy will come to speak death over her, but you will have countered it every time you have spoken her name." I left my prayer closet with a new name for my child, but I could not really fathom the warning I had just received.

Eva had a normal birth story, other than one detail. At the moment her birth was imminent, my doctor gave me a look. I could tell something was going on. He said, "Listen to me, this has to be the last push, okay?" He didn't explain anything, as there was little time to explain.

I simply nodded and replied, "Okay, let's go!"

Little did I know that the umbilical cord was wrapped twice around her neck, tightening with every push. The doctor placed his fingers protectively around her neck, tearing the cord away as I pushed, and Eva was safely delivered. Had the timing been off just a little, that moment could have been fatal—but there was a NEXT.

A year passed, and all was well with our little family. We lived on a few acres of land and loved coming home off the road from our music ministry to the place God had given us. Aaron took care of mowing the grass and cleaning up the outside, while my duties kept me inside cleaning and doing laundry. We were a normal family who enjoyed the simple things of life.

One day in 2008, something happened that caused my mind to travel back to the promise God gave us for Eva. Aaron was washing off his mower and spraying the flowers outside, and our children were running around playing in the water, as most children would. Eva was suddenly covered head-to-toe with hives.

Focus on the Promise

Aaron brought her inside, and I put her in the bathtub, thinking she must have gotten something on her skin. Within seconds, she turned blue and passed out cold. Not taking the time to get cleaned up, we rushed out the door and raced to the hospital.

I left the house in a short gown, and Aaron was wearing jeans with no shirt or shoes. Eli and Eva were naked, wrapped only in towels. We called 911, but we determined that we could make it to our local hospital before the ambulance could get to us.

We prayed and pleaded with God the whole way to the hospital. Eli joined in and said, "Jesus, please help my sister!" Eva appeared lifeless, and her breathing was so shallow it couldn't be heard or felt.

When we arrived at the hospital, they took one look at her and rushed us to the back. The doctors and nurses were working to help her, but nothing was changing. Her blood pressure was very low, and her heartbeat was faint. As they were scrambling, I finally got in her face and said, "Eva, God gave you your name, and He spoke life over you before you were born. Even though the enemy would love to bring death to you, you are life! In Jesus' Name, you will live!"

It felt like time stood still. All of a sudden, Eva gasped for air and sat up in the bed. "Momma!" she screamed. We all rejoiced with a shout of praise in that hospital room. Even the hospital staff joined in our excitement. We later found out that Eva had an allergy to cold. A combination of the cold water outside and the bath water inside triggered an allergic reaction (hives) which resulted in an anaphylactic response (passing out, shock). This was something we had never heard of until it happened to us.

Her life had once again been threatened, but God gave us victory. We felt like we had overcome our worst nightmare, or so we thought. As that day became a distant memory, we continued to give God praise for life. We kept on traveling and ministering every week. Though this season of ministry was tough, it was crucial for what lay ahead. It was the preparation ground for the next phase of our ministry.

AN UNEXPECTED EVENT

When the Crabb Family disbanded, Aaron and I had started our own ministry. We had to purchase sound equipment, microphones, and other items needed to start a small road ministry. We bought a bus, which was not the best decision at the time. Despite all the things going wrong, we were seeing lives being changed, and that was the fuel we needed to keep us moving ahead.

One night, as we were leaving for a long week of ministry, I heard the Lord speak to me again in His gentle yet convicting way. He said, "Go on a fast."

I began to ask the Lord, "How long? Why?" I heard nothing in response. In that moment there was an urgency that came up in my spirit, and I knew I must be obedient. So, the very next day, I started a fast.

One night after a revival meeting, my body became very weak. Aaron said "Amanda, we've got a long week ahead of us, and you've been ministering, pouring out everything you have. You should at least drink broth or something for strength."

NEXT

I looked at him and said these words that have rung in our ears for years: "I feel like if I put one drop of food to my lips, it will change our whole destiny, and I don't know what that even means."

God sometimes will allow us to feel a burden without giving us every detail. If He were to give us the total picture, we would live in fear, when we should be walking in faith. When we walk in faith, we are letting Him guide us each step of the way, instead of manipulating the process ourselves.

The following week was GMA week, or Gospel Music Association week. It was full of meetings, interviews, showcases, and the Dove Awards. I missed my children terribly. The days were long, and we were away from them a lot. And it seemed like when we were home, they were sleeping.

It was Thursday, April 23, 2009, a date that would soon be forever marked in our household. We didn't have to be at the Grand Ole Opry until around 2:00 p.m. for the Dove Awards, so we had some time to spend with Eli and Eva that morning. I cherished it. As we made the bed, Eva came right behind me and tucked her babies in on top of it. She normally would take the babies with her, but this day she gently laid them down, tucked them in. I overheard these words: "Baby, I will come back. I promise you I will!" I looked over at her and thought how sweet this moment was, such an innocent little girl, imitating me and pretending to play "Mommy."

Aaron and I soon left the house and dropped Eli and Eva off with our nanny for the evening. We kissed them goodbye, and we told them, "We promise we will be back in just a few hours." It was just like the way Eva had spoken over her dolls.

The event was rolling along as planned. We finished our portion of the pre-show and were heading into the main event of the night. The time was 7:55 p.m., and the show would begin promptly at 8:00 p.m. We were asked to silence our phones for the rest of the evening, but something pressing inside told me to leave my phone out.

At 8:00 p.m. exactly, my phone rang. I answered quickly and heard our nanny, her voice frantic and hysterical, saying, "Amanda, Eva has fallen out of my window!"

I jumped out of my seat. Aaron could tell by the look on my face that what I just heard was serious. I explained to him what the nanny just told me. He could only ask, "Is she alive?"

My heart sank as I realized that I didn't even know the answer to his question. Our nanny lived in a second story apartment. As you can imagine, a million thoughts were running through my head. A phone call back confirmed that Eva was indeed alive but was covered in blood. I could hear the sirens in the background, and I was grateful to know that help was already there.

When we spoke to the emergency personnel, they told us they would be life-flighting her to the local children's hospital. In our race to get to Eva, we beat the ambulance to the hospital. The staff led us into the room where Eva would arrive. All we could do at that point was pray.

In a few moments, our beautiful two-year-old baby girl was wheeled into the room on a stretcher. Her beautiful hair was no longer blonde, but red, stained by her blood. Again, I was reminded of God's words over Eva. Those words assured me that Eva had a lot of fight in her. In fact, she was fighting with everything in her to get out of the straps and off the stretcher.

The staff tried to sedate her, but the more medicine they gave her, the more agitated she became. The doctors arrived next with their assessments. According to their professional opinion, it looked grim. They informed us of the possibility that her spine might have been severed. They warned us of the potential for brain swelling and seizures. They told us that the days ahead would determine whether she would be able to perform even the most normal activities.

We stood there listening with natural ears, but my spirit rejected their words. I looked at the lead doctor and politely said, "Sir, I respect you and your opinion, but I will tell you that it isn't your report in which I trust. The Lord has placed all of you in this very moment to be a help to my daughter, and if you don't mind, I am going to lay my hands on you and ask for the Great Physician to take over and guide your hands."

We didn't hold anything back in this moment. We prayed and asked for the hand of God to come down over this team of nurses and doctors, and to give them the wisdom needed to help our child. We declared the promises of God that had already been spoken over Eva's life before she ever took her first breath. We declared that she would live and not die, and that she would declare the works of the Lord.

> **We Held Nothing Back**

We intensified our prayers by praying in tongues. The amazing part was that the doctors didn't even flinch. There was no denying that the power of God was in that very room to heal our baby girl. We concluded the prayer by saying; "Father, we thank you that this staff will declare they have seen a miracle tonight!"

They attempted to get the first CT scan, but Eva wasn't having it. She continued to fight them. They wheeled her back into that trauma unit and told us; "Mom and Dad, we are going to clear the room and leave you alone. You're going to have to calm her down so we can finish this process, so we can know what steps we must take next."

As those words were spoken, something inside of me leaped with excitement. I was instantly reminded of a story in the Gospel of Matthew when the little girl had died. When Jesus got to her house, they were mourning and weeping. Doubt filled the room. When Jesus showed up, He told them, "Make room!" Jesus cleared the room so that He could speak and perform a miracle.

We looked at our baby with the top of her head laid open, her mouth filled with blood, and a brace on her neck, yet we had a hope deeper than our sight. We asked her if she wanted us to sing a song to her. After naming off a few of her favorites, the only one she wanted to hear was a worship song that she loved. Together, Aaron and I began to sing and worship God together. It was more than just a song to us; it was an expression of consecration to God and our trust in Him that came from the depths of our hearts.

We never fully understood sacrificial worship until this very moment. This must have been what Abraham felt when he was asked to lay his son Isaac on the altar. With tears streaming down our faces and our hands lifted, the room was empty, and yet it became very crowded. You could feel the presence of heaven in that room. We didn't know what the outcome would be from this tragedy, but right then it didn't matter. We were compelled to worship Him. Somehow, some way, our God would provide himself a lamb. He is, after all, Jehovah Jireh, our Provider, our Savior, and our Deliverer.

When we looked back at our daughter, we saw she had fallen into a deep, deep sleep. The Prince of Peace had given her some much-needed rest.

With Eva no longer fighting and resisting, the doctors were able to get the scan which later showed that there was zero brain or spinal damage to our baby. She would need stitches on her head and surgery in her mouth where her lip had been severed from her jawbone, but that was it. Our God had entered the room and brought her a miraculous healing.

Later, while Eva was undergoing surgery, a detective who had been assigned to investigate the accident spoke with us. He also questioned our son Eli, as well as our niece who had been staying with the nanny. Grueling questions were asked, and accusations were made. The detective wanted to arrest our nanny for neglect and child endangerment. When we told him we were not going to press charges against the nanny, he began to question what type of parents we were.

Although Eli and our niece had told him that our nanny had only left the room to grab Eva's diaper bag, he and his colleagues were trying to paint a much different story. As a result, Aaron and I were now under investigation by child services, with the threat of being declared unfit parents. We heard comments such as, "Maybe you don't deserve to have these children."

We looked at them and said, "We have nothing to hide. You're welcome to place surveillance on us if that is what is needed." Aaron and I knew God was greater than these accusations.

Back in the waiting room, our family members had gathered to support us. They told us that thousands of people were standing with us in prayer. Immediately, Aaron looked at me and we realized that this was why I had been fasting. It had been nine days since I had eaten one bite of food. The sacrifice of food set the standard that had been raised against the enemy.

God allowed us to have a preemptive strike against the enemy—which in turn saved Eva's life. He had known the attack was coming, and He had drawn the battle lines. He brought us a great victory that day. As we were being discharged after Eva's recovery from surgery, the lead doctor said, "Mrs. Crabb, it's just like you prayed—we have seen a miracle today!"

I felt strange fasting and not being able to see what was ahead. Sometimes, though, the things that seem the strangest to our natural mind are the very things that bring us supernatural victories.

The men in our opening story had to carry someone into a room full of spectators who were only there taking up space. They got creative in the process by making a hole in a roof, just to get him to Jesus. This must have appeared foolish to most, until this same man who was lowered through the roof picked up his bed and began to walk.

Don't think it is strange when the Lord asks you to do something that makes no sense to your natural mind. It is only a sign that there is a greater NEXT in store for you and those you love. When He prompted me to go on a fast (especially for nine days!), fasting was not even on my radar, and I did think it was strange. We have learned that often the stranger the direction from God, the greater the NEXT in our lives.

Eva fell fifteen feet out of a second-story window and hit an air conditioning unit. Today, she has a powerful anointing on her life to worship. A prophetic word was recently spoken over her that the reason she hit an air conditioning unit that day was because she has an anointing to change the temperature in a room. It is true, her presence does just that. When she worships, it shifts the atmosphere. Truly, what the enemy meant for harm, our God meant for a NEXT.

Chapter Three

OBEDIENCE

Has the LORD as great delight in burnt offerings and sacrifices, As in obeying the voice of the LORD? Behold, to obey is better than sacrifice, And to heed than the fat of rams.

1 Samuel 15:22

FROM THE DESK OF AARON:

I was in a crowd of people, staring into a pit so black I couldn't see the bottom. Looking around, I saw a rope hanging over the side, with people clinging to it as if it were a lifeline. They were screaming, "Help me, help me!"

I had gone into my closet to spend some time praying and suddenly found myself immersed in a vision from God.

In the vision, there were plenty of people watching, but no one was willing to pull those crying for help out of the deep, dark pit. It surprised me, so I began pulling on the rope. One by one, they began to climb out of the pit. Once out of the pit, they were instantly transformed from their dirty attire into their Sunday best. Clutching Bibles in their hands, they began walking toward a church.

As I watched the action unfold, the scene shifted. I saw myself on a platform in a church. I was preaching the gospel

33

and the altars were quickly filling up with people. Amanda and our son, Eli, were laying hands on people and praying for them. Eva was there, too, working in the church.

IT'S BETTER TO OBEY

This vision came to pass five years ago when we planted Restoring Hope Church in Hendersonville, Tennessee. We are still in complete awe of the work the Lord is doing here. He has used this church to pull many people out of a place of darkness, hopelessness, and despair into a brighter tomorrow and a God-given destiny.

The shift from the vision to the reality did not come overnight. I tried to make the vision what I wanted it to be. Initially, we moved to a large, well-known church in San Antonio where I became a worship pastor. I was comfortable with music, but slowly began to realize that music was only part of the process, not the fulfilment of the vision. After five years of serving as the worship pastor, God began to deal with me.

He asked me, "Aaron, when are you going to be obedient to what I have shown you?"

I knew that being obedient to God meant submitting to His authority in my life. I wasn't ready to do that...yet. I told God, "I'm not qualified. I don't have what it takes; I'm not prepared or set up for that yet."

From that moment, I started to become miserable. My perfect marriage of eight years began to unravel. We faced financial hardships, and arguments began to surface. Nothing seemed to be working in our relationship. As a result, I found myself just going through the motions. I went to work, but I stopped communicating with Amanda.

One day I was sitting in my backyard, staring at a large tree, whose roots were pushing up out of the ground. The tree looked old, as if it might be dying. God spoke to me and said, "This is how you feel, right? On the outside you appear mighty and strong, but on the inside, you feel dead."

I replied with a simple, "Yes."

God drew my attention to the bottom of the tree, where some green limbs were showing. He said, "There is still life in that tree, and there is still life in you. Peel back the layers and find Aaron again."

I said "Yes, Lord!"

It wasn't much longer after this response that my family and I were led back to Hendersonville, Tennessee, where we planted Restoring Hope Church. Amanda and I had no idea how to plant a church, but we realized that God didn't call us to be comfortable; He called us to be obedient.

When I think of obedience, I am reminded of the story in 2 Kings 5. Naaman was the commander of the army for the King of Syria. He was a great and honorable man in the eyes of his king. He was a mighty man of valor and had brought great victory to Syria, but he had a problem: he was a leper.

We are not perfect. Even great men and women are not perfect. Regardless of how strong we are, we all face situations and conflicts in life. Not only do we have imperfections, but God can use those imperfections to perform His perfect work.

NEXT

We don't have to be without fault or feebleness for God to use us. Paul said, "His strength is made perfect in my weaknesses." We don't have to answer a questionnaire or pass a spiritual exam to be saved. The Bible says in Romans 10:13, "*For whoever calls on the name of the LORD shall be saved.*" For those who are wrestling with issues, my prayer is that you will find strength through the name of Jesus Christ to believe for your NEXT.

Naaman was a great man not only because he was a warrior, but also because he was willing to admit he had a problem. This is key for finding our NEXT. Luke 11:28 says, "*More than that, blessed are those who hear the word of God and keep it!*"

One day, Naaman heard from an Israelite servant girl that there was a prophet in Israel who could heal him.

Many people in this kind of lowly position would have been happy to take notice of their captor's illness, but not this girl. Instead, she expressed incredible spirit. She desired Naaman's well-being. She exemplified what Jesus taught His disciples: "*But I say to you, love your enemies, bless those who curse you, do good to those who hate you, and pray for those who spitefully use you and persecute you*" (Matthew 5:44).

Others may have enjoyed watching their enemy sick and suffering, but she told Naaman how he could find healing. She directed him to the prophet of Israel and to the power of the Word of God.

One of the most important things in life is to know where the power is. We must direct our focus on the Word of God; it is His Word that will produce the power. And His Word says, "*But He was wounded for our transgressions, He was bruised for our iniquities; The chastisement for our peace was upon Him, And by His stripes we are healed"* (Isaiah 53:5).

Neither padded pews nor the best sound equipment will ever add up to power. Smoke and lights won't usher in the presence of God. Nor will wearing a five-pound cross around your neck, having the Bible app on your phone, or displaying the family Bible on the coffee table give you any special status in the Kingdom of God. You can have great talent, great skill, and great recognition among men, but no power. Your NEXT will not be based on prestige, but on power—God's power.

Where's the Power?

The Apostle Paul said, "*... I will come to you shortly, if the Lord wills, and I will know, not the word of those who are puffed up, but the power. For the kingdom of God is not in word but in power*" (1 Corinthians 4:19-20). The power of the kingdom is the power of the blood, the power of the cross, and the power of the resurrected Christ.

Naaman told the King of Syria what the servant girl had said. He quickly wrote a letter to the King of Israel, saying that he was sending Naaman to him to be healed. The King of Israel took offense at the letter, interpreting it as an effort on the Syrian king's part to start a quarrel. He said, "Am I God, that I can heal this man? He is just trying to pick a fight with me!" Rather than admit that he was powerless to heal Naaman, he accused the King of Syria of being a troublemaker.

The King of Israel was powerless to heal anyone; he shifted the blame.

When religion cannot produce, it shifts the blame.

NEXT

Religion can never substitute for the reality of relationship. Relationship will say, "It's my fault. I'm not where I need to be with God."

Relationship will say, "I'm sorry I haven't been praying and fasting like I should."

Relationship will say, "I'm sorry. The problem isn't with God, and it isn't with you—the problem is with me."

As it happened, Elisha the prophet overheard the King of Israel's lament. Elisha had a relationship with God. He said, "Don't worry, King. Send him to me, and he will find out there is a prophet in Israel."

Little did Naaman know that Elisha was preparing to show him the difference between trusting in a man, even though he was a prophet, and trusting in God himself. He was about to be redirected toward his NEXT.

Sometimes God has to redirect our faith. Naaman had faith, faith enough to get him moving, but he assumed that power was with position. He assumed that those who had power with men also had power with God. But it is only a relationship with God that can release results and move us into our NEXT.

THE HEART OF THE MATTER

So Naaman arrived at the prophet's home. Elisha decided not to meet him personally, but to send out a messenger. This would not go over well in the church of today, but we must understand that God's ways are not always our ways.

God, through the process of purpose, will push out pride. This was the first blow to Naaman. I can imagine him thinking, *"Am I not a great man? The prophet should have met me himself instead of sending a lowly servant!"* The second blow came after the messenger tells him to go dip seven times in the muddy Jordan River and he would be healed.

Naaman thought Elisha would come out, wave his hand over his skin, and he would be healed. As a result, he became angry because he had his own preconceived idea of how he would receive his healing. So many times, we have our own ideas of how God will do something. We have it all worked out. We know how we want God to do it, when we want Him to do it, where we want Him to do it, and who we want Him to use to do it.

I tried to make the vision God had given me happen when I moved my family to San Antonio, Texas. As it turned out, that was not the place the vision was supposed to be fulfilled.

The truth of the matter is that God is preparing us on the inside for what He wants to do on the outside. We can be so quick to let God see the surface issues, the stuff that doesn't really matter, but to change the flesh, we have got to get to the root cause of the problem.

God is concerned with our flesh, but He is more concerned with the root of our problems: our heart. Yes, He is concerned with fixing our money problems, our unhealthy habits, our relationships; He is more concerned with healing our hearts because in the heart lies the source of our problems.

NEXT

God wants to remove unforgiveness, anger, bitterness, jealousy, envy, strife, rebellion, and pride. Pride was what was killing Naaman. He had leprosy in his body, but pride was destroying his soul. Before Naaman could be healed of the disease in his body, he first had to be delivered from the disease in his soul. Proverbs 4:23 says, *"Keep your heart with all diligence, For out of it spring the issues of life."* We cannot get to our NEXT without healing what lies in our hearts.

> **Keep Your Heart with All Diligence**

Naaman's pride asked the question, "Why do I have to go dip seven times in the muddy Jordan, when there are beautiful, clean rivers where I come from?"

When God spoke to me about moving back to Tennessee and planting a church, I remembered asking myself a similar question: *Why would I go back and start a church from nothing—no building, no congregation, no money to support it—when I am a part of one of the largest, most effective churches in America?*

Why would I leave a steady income, an incredible school for my children, and an amazing studio for producing music to go start a brand-new church on nothing but a word? But it is God's Word that holds the power to produce His promise.

Seven is my favorite number. Seven also is a Biblical number and means completion. The number seven was significant for Naaman, since the prophet had instructed him to dip seven times in the Jordan River. He could not receive his healing unless he obeyed the instructions.

Sometimes we wonder why we haven't received everything we need from God. The answer may be that we have only partially done what God has asked. *Partially* won't work; when God says seven times, five or six times won't do. If Naaman would have stopped at four, five or even six times, his healing would not have occurred, and there would have been no manifestation of God's power.

It's easier to obey God when it makes sense to us, when it doesn't make us look silly, or when it's convenient and comfortable. I have found in my own life that in order to receive the blessing of God, it will cost me something. It will cost me more than money; it will cost me my obedience.

Each dip in the water stripped pride from Naaman's heart. Obeying God will cost us our pride, our plans, and our personal ideas. It will cost us our feelings and emotions. What I admire about Naaman is that he relented and kept dipping until he had finished what he had been instructed to do. He understood commitment, and he understood perseverance. Most importantly, he understood that he could not let his pride stand in the way of receiving his healing.

We need this type of commitment and understanding, if we are to move forward into our NEXT. Obedient perseverance wins the prize. God will show us His purpose and promise for our lives, but He never promised that it would be easy or quick.

My desire is to propel you into action. If God has told you to do something, and these words stir in your heart, then simply move in obedience. Don't think about it, talk about it, or meditate on it. Just obey. When you move forward in obedience, your natural human ability will intersect with the supernatural power of a miracle-working God, and you will see the manifestation of His glory.

Like the poor widow woman who was gathering sticks to light a fire and bake a cake for her and her son to eat and then die, you will experience the power and provision of God. The prophet told her, "Make me a cake first, and your meal barrel will not be empty, and your cruse of oil will not run dry." When she obeyed the word of the Lord, she was sustained through the famine in a way she had never thought possible.

Obey God even if it doesn't make sense. You are one act of obedience away from a release of God's supernatural miracle-working power. Why would Naaman go all the way to the prophet's home in Israel to hear God's voice, then turn around and leave because it didn't happen the way he expected it to happen? He didn't give up and leave, and neither should you.

Don't allow anything to cheat you out of the blessings of God. Don't allow your pride, your fear, or what people might think or say about you to rob you of your victory, your healing, your joy. Don't allow your feelings, your emotions, or your disobedience to get in the way. Obey the word of the Lord, and watch God move you into your NEXT.

Chapter Four

THROUGH THE PRESS

Brethren, I do not count myself to have apprehended; but one thing I do, forgetting those things which are behind and reaching forward to those things which are ahead, I press toward the goal for the prize of the upward call of God in Christ Jesus.

Philippians 3:13-14

FROM THE DESK OF AMANDA:

Aaron and I were both raised in Kentucky, so we cannot help but be basketball fans. It is in our DNA. We love everything about basketball: the cheering of the crowd, the squeak of the players' shoes on the floor, the sound of the referee's whistle. Not only can watching two highly ranked basketball teams play against each other deliver a healthy dose of excitement, but it can also be accompanied by the realization of a life lesson.

There is a mode of defense called the *full court press*. Defensive players often allow the offensive team to get halfway down the court before defensive pressure is applied—the *half court press*. A full court press is a defensive style in which the defense applies pressure to the offensive team the entire length of the court from the moment the ball comes into play. Pressure may be applied man-to-man or by using a zone defense.

This is a great system if you are the one playing defense. However, it creates a very frustrating situation if you are the one trying to make it to the goal. The closer you get to the basket, the tougher the defense becomes. Is this not a picture of life?

We have often heard these words from God-fearing believers: "Why is life so hard? Why does it feel like the closer I get to my goal, the tougher the resistance becomes?"

Our answer is always the same. We have an adversary, an opponent who does not want us to win. But we can't stop moving—the pressure is just an indication that breakthrough is at hand!

There was a woman whose story is told in Luke 8:43-48. She was in desperate need of healing and was trying to get to Jesus. The press of people crowding around Him kept her from touching Him; she could only get close enough to touch His clothing. Her faith said that was enough; even though she did not touch Him, her faith did. She was healed immediately.

Despite the crowd around Him, Jesus noticed it right away. He felt the release of healing power as her faith connected. She had pushed past the press of people and received her healing.

I have heard these sayings all my life:

- *The tougher the battle, the sweeter the victory.*
- *Nothing worth having comes easy.*
- *The more you struggle to achieve something, the less likely you will be to take it for granted.*

While all these statements are true, they don't make you feel any better when you are in the middle of the struggle, and all you can think about is quitting. Let's face it, even the strongest Christians have bad days. I would love to tell you that I have never entertained the thought of giving up. But I have thought it, and I have even said it—I just never acted on it.

We must keep pressing forward toward our NEXT. We can't allow ourselves to become stuck in a place of complacency and defeat. There is hope, healing, and a future in front of us.

STRATEGIZE A PLAN

In those moments of weakness, we have to learn what to do. We cannot afford to isolate ourselves. Isolation is one of the main tools that our enemy will use. If he can change our mentality to be one of *me, myself, and I,* then we will lose the desire to see beyond ourselves. If he can get us to think only about ourselves and our problems, he can rob us of a vital source of strength and support.

Alone, we become insecure, easily offended, and our soul wounds begin to fester with infection. They need to be exposed so that oxygen can bring healing. While it is not good to be alone, it is equally important that we don't connect with the wrong people. It is easy to team up with people who think, talk, and act just like us.

The truth is that while we are still a work-in-progress, we need someone who can talk us out of our pit and not someone who will settle into the pit with us. We don't need an ear to listen to us; we need a God-ordained mouthpiece to speak truth into our lives. We need someone who will help us get to the goal to make the winning shot.

As we grow in God's kingdom, we will become less concerned about who gets the credit and more concerned about the win for the entire body. The strategy for overcoming the full court press of the enemy is to have someone closer to the goal than we are to help us get the shot. When we start feeling the pressure, it's time to start looking for a teammate who can shoulder some of the heavy load for a moment.

DISCOVER YOUR GIFTING

The body of Christ is a team. Therefore, we must act like a team. We all have different gifts, and yet they all work together. We have a saying at our church: *stay in your lane.* It is important to know our gifting. God has given us specific gifts, for a specific purpose. The beautiful thing about this purpose is that we don't have to get there alone. There will always be someone to help us achieve our goal.

Aaron and I have four beautiful children. Each one is unique in their own way. Elijah, our first born, has a prophetic anointing like his namesake. Ever since he was little, he has been able to foretell things to come, and they would happen. Sometimes this gift is a blessing, and sometimes, well, it still needs to be corralled. With the prophetic anointing comes a strong opinion and a strong sense of truth. He is learning daily that this gift is nothing if it isn't wrapped in the love of Christ.

He is wise beyond his years, and while he is still finding his footing, the unfolding of his gift is a beautiful process to behold. He is like a diamond in the rough. Once he fully understands the magnitude of the authority given to him, he will be a force to be reckoned with against the rulers of darkness.

Eva brings life. She creates, writes, designs, and sings. We have cards all over our home filled with words of encouragement and love. She takes the soft approach to ministry, filled with deep conviction. I often hear people say that if they need prayer, Eva is the first one they ask. She knows how to get ahold of God. She understands that prayer moves mountains.

Ean is full of joy. His name means "God is good." He truly has one of the most contagious smiles of anyone I have ever met. Ean was born in a season when we really needed joy. He was born at a transitional time that sometimes felt rocky and unsettled. No matter how bad a day we are having, he can fill the room with joy with just one smile. He is the child that I would take to the doctor for a regular checkup only to find out that he had a double ear infection. He just smiled through the pain.

Eda is our last song. T. F. Tenney prophesied over Aaron and I one night in 2015. He said, "Now listen, You two are going to birth one more song. In fact, it is in the conception stage even now." He said that when this song was birthed, everyone would be blessed, and they will know they have heard from God.

Aaron walked away excited, thinking that we were going to pen a powerful melody, comparable to "The Name of Jesus." I said, "Honey, I don't get the feeling he's speaking of an actual song at all."

That was Thursday, and by Saturday night we found out our little songbird was closer than we expected. Her life verse is Proverbs 10:22: *"The blessing of the LORD makes one rich, And He adds no sorrow with it."* She is truly a blessing to everyone who meets and knows her. She has the same tenacity as her big brother, Elijah. We often need to corral her, too. Her name means "happy, healthy warrior," and I am thankful she has those qualities.

The Blessing of the Lord Makes Rich

Each child's gifts work together beautifully within our family, as well as in our ministry. Each one different, but they have the same purpose. For Fathers' Day 2017, Eva decided to make a card, exercising her unique gifts. When Ean saw that she was going to be making something special, he wanted in on it, too—but he needed his big sister's help.

Elijah was not into cardmaking; he just walked up to his father and said, "I love and appreciate you, Dad. Happy Father's Day!" Simple as that.

The cardmaking continued with the two middle kids in the dining room. Ean asked Eva for help in spelling *Father's Day*. Ever the helpful sister, she broke it down for him in three syllables to make it easier for him to write.

The time came to reveal their hard labor of love to dad. Eva's card was filled with deep expressions. She thanked him for being a man of compassion and love. She thanked him for being a man of integrity full of the wisdom of God. She told him how grateful she was that he taught his family how to love Jesus. She told him how much she appreciated him stepping out in faith and starting Restoring Hope

Church. We were in a puddle of tears reading her card. Her gift was in full operation. She affirmed the wellspring of life inside her father; his labor had not been in vain but was accomplishing everything he envisioned.

As Aaron dried his tears, Ean stood all smiles ready to move his daddy with his card. As Aaron took the card from our eager little boy, he saw what Ean had written on the front of the card. In large, childlike letters it read: "HAPPY FAT. HERS. DAY."

We laughed uncontrollably at how sweet and cute it was. But Ean's smile quickly turned to tears. He couldn't understand how Eva's sentiment moved us one way and his another. He said, "Wow! Eva makes you cry, and you laugh at me?" What had been a joyous filled moment quickly turned to gloom as Ean took off running up the stairs.

Without a moment's thought, I followed Ean, intent on correcting him. I said "You come here, young man. I want to explain something to you. You and Eva have very different giftings. She used her gift to bless daddy, and it moved him one way.

"But your gift to us is joy. You have always brought happiness and smiles into an atmosphere that is heavy. God gave us the gift of laughter through you today. We weren't making fun of you; we absolutely loved it! Listen to me. You will not compare yourself to others in your life. You are called to be different, and you will not live offended. Do you hear me, Ean William? You will not walk in offense!"

He politely shook his head, and said, "Yes, ma'am." I hugged him and told him how much we loved him.

He said, "I love you, too, Mom." Then he waited for a few seconds, and said, "Mom, can I ask you something?" He had a deep puzzled look on his face.

I said, "Sure honey, what is it?"

He said, "What if one day I have to walk *through* a *fence*?

I couldn't help but chuckle. "Oh, my sweet Ean, if you walk *through* it, you will be just fine."

This precious seven-year-old had pictured a fence and being stuck behind that fence forever. What a profound thought. Many of us live life being stuck. The victory is so close, and yet here we are refusing to walk through the fence. Instead, we find ourselves daily walking into the same old, same old thing that is continually hurting us and holding us back.

We cannot look at the giftings of others and think, "Well, I can't do it like that," or "I don't move people with my gift the way that person does."

News flash: We're not supposed to. Each one of us has a special purpose, and the number one thing we are to do is honor our Father with the gifts He has blessed us with. We all need to have the same thought as Ean and declare, "I am walking through it! I will not walk *in* a *fence*, but I will walk *through* it!"

There will be days we will be offended. There will be days we will feel hurt and rejected when the enemy has come against us full force. His main purpose is to keep us behind the fence, not advancing, and not moving closer to the goal. He wants us to believe that we have

> Keep
> Advancing

nothing to offer in this thing called life, but that is a lie. We must refuse to believe it any longer!

How do I know what my gifting is?

I love the taking inventory tests that ask questions and give results based on what you have answered. But I feel that depending on our mood that day, those results may vary. I believe we often won't know what our true gifting is until we start moving in it and start walking through it.

Had we never ever explained to Ean that his gift was joy, he may not have realized why his card moved us to laughter. Had it not been for his big sister spelling out those three syllables for him, he may not have had the opportunity to understand how one gift can facilitate another; she was being a help to him in that moment.

We can't allow the enemy to take what is intended to press us forward into our destiny and use it to keep us behind boundary lines for the rest of our lives. We can't let ourselves become offended and remain stagnant.

The basketball players who feel the effect of the defensive press are the offensive players. The offensive players are the ones in possession of the ball. Even though the press is coming against them, they know that the team who holds the ball, holds the power.

They just keep moving forward against the press; they don't stop advancing. Their strategy to defeat the press is speed—they move quickly, and they work together.

As Christians, our strategy against the press of life is to be quick as well—quick to forgive, quick to love, quick to show kindness to a stranger, and quick to support our fellow teammates when we are in the heat of the press. We are all in it together. There must be unity.

Life is often like a game of basketball. There may only be five players on the court doing the work at any specific time, but each player is still part of the team. Each player has a specific role and a specific responsibility.

If we find ourselves seated on the sidelines for a season, we shouldn't give up because our time to play hasn't come yet. We are still on the team. We must be faithful where we are and keep cheering the entire team on. We never know when the BIG coach is going to put us in NEXT!

Chapter Five

THE LAST STOP

For the children of Israel walked forty years in the wilderness, till all the people who were men of war, who came out of Egypt, were consumed, because they did not obey the voice of the LORD—to whom the LORD swore that He would not show them the land which the LORD had sworn to their fathers that He would give us, "a land flowing with milk and honey." Then Joshua circumcised their sons whom He raised up in their place; for they were uncircumcised, because they had not been circumcised on the way.

So it was, when they had finished circumcising all the people, that they stayed in their places in the camp till they were healed. Then the LORD said to Joshua, "This day I have rolled away the reproach of Egypt from you." Therefore the name of the place is called Gilgal to this day. Now the children of Israel camped in Gilgal, and kept the Passover on the fourteenth day of the month at twilight on the plains of Jericho. And they ate of the produce of the land on the day after the Passover, unleavened bread and parched grain, on the very same day. Then the manna ceased on the day after they had eaten the produce of the land; and the children of Israel no longer had manna, but they ate the food of the land of Canaan that year.

And it came to pass, when Joshua was by Jericho, that he lifted his eyes and looked, and behold, a Man stood opposite him with His sword drawn in His hand. And Joshua went to Him and said to Him, "Are You for us or for our adversaries?"

So He said, "No, but as Commander of the army of the LORD I have now come."

And Joshua fell on his face to the earth and worshiped, and said to Him, "What does my Lord say to His servant?"

Then the Commander of the LORD's army said to Joshua, "Take your sandal off your foot, for the place where you stand is holy." And Joshua did so.

Joshua 5:6-15

FROM THE DESK OF AARON:

I t was the very last day the bill could be paid. No money had come in, and the payment on our church buildings was now due. We filled out the check and told our assistant to run it downtown in faith, believing that God would make a way. I went into my prayer closet and began to pray. I remember saying to God, "This wasn't my idea. This was Your will and Your call, and I need You to move now."

As I was praying, God had shown me a picture of a postman's hand reaching into our mailbox at the church and putting in a $20,000 check.

As I got up from my time of prayer, the phone rang. I answered it right away, only to hear a concerned voice on the other end asking, "What are you going to do?"

I answered, "I have a plan, but I truly believe God is about to make a way."

Those words had no sooner left my mouth than Amanda came running through the house, cell phone in hand. "Aaron!" she said. Her voice was full of energy and excitement.

"It's the office, and it's here!"

A check had arrived at 4:15 p.m., a time when the mail wasn't even supposed to run. This was all God—no man can get the glory. He supplied the money to show us who He is; His actions proved to us how big our God is. He is Jehovah Jireh, our Provider!

BETWEEN HERE AND THERE

The book of Joshua is a mighty display of the overcoming power and authority of God. It is a book that will fuel your faith when you are about to slay your enemy and take possession of your promise. It is a book that will inspire you to do something you have never done before. It is a book that will invigorate you and assure you that God is with you; He is the same yesterday, today and forever.

It is also a book of perspective. When God is moving, there will be demonic spirits working overtime to divert, entangle, stagnate and immobilize you.

The Word is clear that we are engaged in a supernatural battle while living in a natural world: *"For though we walk in the flesh, we do not war after the flesh: For the weapons of our warfare are not carnal but mighty in God for pulling down strongholds"* (2 Corinthians 10:3-4).

NEXT

We can see that God revealed Himself to the Israelites time after time. He brought the mothers and fathers of this people out of Egypt's bondage. The signs and wonders were absolutely beyond belief, yet the people who saw so much of God's goodness and generosity still failed to enter into His fullness. So many died in the wilderness—right next door to what they set out to obtain.

God blessed them and invested so much in them. He fought off their enemies by releasing boils and frogs. He turned water into blood. He sent a north wind to blow back the Red Sea so that the children of Israel could walk across on dry ground.

When their enemies tried to follow God's people into their future, God drowned them right in the midst of the sea.

Do you feel as though you have been haunted by the enemies of your past? Be assured that God has drowned your past in the depths of the Red Sea of His blood never to be remembered again. It has been forgiven and forgotten forever. Amen!

As the sea closed over their enemies, the Israelites celebrated in triumph. Miriam played her tambourine, the people danced, and they all watched as God gave them the victory.

There is nothing quite like watching God defeat the principalities arrayed against you that will make you move, shout, dance, cry tears of joy, clap your hands, or even sing a song of praise. Maybe you shouldn't even be alive and well and reading this book today, but God protected you, healed you or provided for you, just like He protected, healed and provided for the Israelites.

When they came to the bitter waters of Marah (which represented the bitterness and complaining spirit that was inside of them), He healed the stream and made it sweet.

In the wilderness of Sin, He rained manna from heaven so that the people would know that He was God.

When they were encamped at Rephidim, He sent water out of a rock.

It is amazing to me that the God of the universe did all these things for a people who remained unthankful. He brought the Israelites out of and through so many things.

If anyone were going to believe God, it should have been this generation. But they forgot all that from which He had previously delivered them and did not really believe that He would do what He said He would do. They heard the Word, but they did not believe the Word. They saw the miracles, but still did not believe in the power of Almighty God.

They Saw the Miracles

Because of their unbelief, all but two of them died in the wilderness. Hebrews 11:6 says, *"But without faith it is impossible to please Him, for he who comes to God must believe that He is, and that He is a rewarder of those who diligently seek Him."*

I am convinced that God will perform mighty acts today to show you who He is and to prove to you that He is still able to deliver.

NEXT

Here is how I know: After we had initiated our church plant, God began to turn our attention to two buildings located on Center Point Road in Hendersonville, Tennessee. Up until then, we had been holding our services at the Hendersonville site of TBN.

The Center Point Road buildings had been sitting empty for three years. There had been 12 offers made that had not been accepted. When we pulled into the parking lot, we said, "Lord, if this is what you desire for Restoring Hope Church, then You will make the way, and they will take our offer." Ours was a lease purchase offer, and they had already turned down cash offers.

But just a few days later, we received their response: "Yes, we will take it!"

The terms of this lease purchase were that we would make our regular monthly payments, which were not cheap, followed by a large payment every October for the next four years.

The first two years, the payments were mainly funded from outside help and fundraisers. In the second year, we hit what felt like a Red Sea. We had half of the money, but we were waiting on the other half. We knew that God had said He would provide.

"What if the money doesn't come in? The bill has to be paid or we will lose the whole contract—and ultimately the building." These thoughts and others crowded my mind.

It was at this point—with a deadline looming and a crisis approaching—that I had entered my prayer closet to intercede for the future of our church.

It was there that God met me, between the promise and the provision, where our faith intersected with our need. In that place, He showed me a *vision* of His *provision*: the postman with the check in his hand! He showed me that the battle was not mine, but His.

God is the one who brought me out of combat and swung it around on my behalf. It was God who spoke to my position, and it instantaneously changed.

I don't care what it looks like, He is the God of the impossible. He's the God who parts the waters. He is the God who provides in the desert. He is the all sufficient, all knowing One, the One who is ever present.

The scripture passage at the opening of this chapter is about the children of those who missed the promise, the sons and daughters of those who escaped bondage. They were the generation born between two locations—between their past and their promise.

They were not where their parents started, but they were not yet living in their destiny. They were between *this* place and *that* place.

Some of you right now may be between sickness and healing, between an exit and an entrance, or between brokenness and blessedness. You are not where you were, but you are not where you are going; you are on a testing ground. The *in-between* is where the enemy will always try to spoil the blessing, but he cannot stop what God is going to do.

What you are facing in this moment can shake you, or it can make you scream out to God. When you are in a big battle, remember you are reaching out to a big God. Have you ever been in an emergency and you needed a *now* God in your *now* situation? You did not pray a fancy learned prayer; you prayed with passion from a place of desperation. It was an earnest expression, an aggressive approach to the throne of God. It was a "Thou son of David, have mercy on me!" kind of prayer.

This in-between generation was in a place where they truly did not know how to reach their place of promise. Their situation had taken them beyond what they knew, and they had not been prepared for that position.

READY TO ENTER IN

So many times, I have felt unprepared for the position God placed me in—just like that generation of Israelites. I don't need faith for the things I can do in my own strength. I need faith for those times that I am in a situation where I have no power of my own to make something happen. I know that faith activates power in my impossible situations.

And so, this in-between generation found themselves in Gilgal. They couldn't enter their promise by themselves. For them, Gilgal was the last stop before the Promised Land. It was the last stop before the Battle of Jericho. They were on the edge of their miracle, on the threshold of their breakthrough, right at their point of victory.

But there was something between them and their promise: this generation had not been circumcised. They had come to the edge of their promise only to discover this obstacle standing in their way. In order to enter into the promise, they had to enter into the covenant. For them, circumcision was the symbol of their covenant with God (Genesis 17:13).

God brought the Israelites to Gilgal—to undergo the covenant of circumcision—where their flesh would be cut away, and they would be prepared to receive their promise. They should have already undergone circumcision; Joshua had to do what their fathers had not done.

Like them, when we get to the edge of our promise, we have to confront whatever it is that is standing between us and victory. Before we can reach our place of promise, God may require us to leave some fleshly desire behind.

We may have to conquer a generational curse that we never dealt with or fully conquered. The wound may hurt, and the cutting away of our flesh might be painful, but our flesh has to die. Generational curses that are hindering our progress must be renounced.

If anger is the effect of the curse, let God work on it. If bitterness has taken root, let God cut it out. Depression cannot go where we are going. Allow God to move you to your own Gilgal so you can completely heal and make it to your place of promise.

God has something new, but it will always come from a place of discomfort. Your NEXT will never come in through the safe zone. If we are in an uncomfortable situation, hold on because something good is about to happen. It might appear crazy and impossible, but nothing is impossible with God. All things are possible to those who believe.

NEXT

God has a strategy for the wounded and the hurting. If you will only listen to His counsel, you will obtain His promise. The promise is yours. The NEXT is yours, and when He says go, start walking towards it. After they recovered from circumcision and arrived at Jericho, God told His people to start walking around the city's wall. As they started walking, they would obtain the victory—one step at a time. You may not have the strength to fight, but move, walk in faith, put one foot in front of the other, and believe God is able to do what He says.

> **The Promise Is Yours**

Chapter Six

HEAR, SPEAK, AND SEE

So then faith comes by hearing, and hearing by the word of God.

Romans 10:17

FROM THE DESK OF AMANDA:

All the children in the room began to squeal and squirm. Some of them even let out small cries of terror. The reptile handlers had brought out a snake for the group of children to view. Aaron and I had taken our two middle children to the Nashville zoo. We were in the reptile and amphibian house where the children were having an up close and personal experience with a few choice animals.

The handler quickly tucked the snake behind his back. He put his finger to his lips and motioned for the children to be quiet. He whispered, "Boys and girls, you have to be very, very quiet while we have this snake out of its cage."

Then he said, "Did you know that snakes don't have ears?"

What? You could see this question in the children's eyes.

"Then why do we need to be so quiet?" one of the children asked.

NEXT

Aaron and I looked at each other. This was something we had not thought about before. We leaned in closer as the handler now had our full attention.

He brought the snake out from behind his back and said, "Snakes do not have ears, but they can feel the vibrations of your voices in the atmosphere. When you get too loud and too rowdy, it terrifies the snake. If there is too much noise, the snake is not able to distinguish what the sounds mean or where they are coming from. We will have to put it back in its cage."

Aaron and I were standing in the corner holding back a Holy Ghost shout. We could hardly contain our excitement about the information we had just heard. Throughout scripture, our adversary is referred to as a serpent. We are hearing that the serpent is terrified by the sound of our voice! Our voice is a powerful weapon, and now we knew why: the sound of our voice released into the atmosphere has the ability to terrify our enemy!

A PLEASING AROMA

Sounds are important. They help us identify what is happening in the world around us.

In the stillness of the night, we might hear the sound of the wind rustling in the treetops. On a stormy night, we might hear the churning of the waves in the ocean. In the early hours of the morning, we might hear the gentle whimpering of a newborn baby.

But natural sounds are not the only way we receive information. We can also receive information from the Spirit of God.

64

In the natural, silence means we are alone. However, in the spirit, we are never alone. Even though we may see and hear destruction and negativity all around us—and the flesh wants us to believe that our God has forsaken us—we know that our God is always with us.

As believers, we must not live according to what we see or what we feel. Our eyes will deceive us, and our heart will fail us, but the Spirit of the living God will lead and guide us into all truth. John 16:13 states, *"However, when He, the Spirit of truth, has come, He will guide you into all truth; for He will not speak on His own authority, but whatever He Hears He will speak; and He will tell you things to come."*

The Spirit of God will speak what He hears to our spiritual ears. We have a requirement to be alert to the sounds entering our ear gate. What we hear, we will speak, and what we speak creates the atmosphere around us.

If our hearing influences our speaking, and our speaking influences the atmosphere—the pervading tone or environment around us—then we can choose what *tone* we will live in. The word *pervading* is an interesting word. It is often used to describe the way a scent is diffused into a room—a pervading odor.

What does the air around us smell like?

It is time to purify the air in which we live. We have the power of the risen Savior living inside of us. Second Corinthians 2:14-15 says, *"Now thanks be to God who always leads us in triumph in Christ, and through us diffuses the fragrance of His knowledge in every place. For we are to God the fragrance of Christ among those who are being saved and*

Triumph In Christ

among those who are perishing." Are we doing our part as Christ-followers—being a sweet-smelling aroma—carrying the scent of Christ everywhere we go? I don't know if you are feeling convicted while you are reading this, but I sure am while I am writing it. What does my life smell like? What aroma am I creating?

It is interesting that what we hear becomes what we speak, what we speak becomes what we smell, what we smell becomes how we feel, and how we feel becomes how we see. This process begins at the gate of hearing. While I may not be able to prove this scientifically, this is the way the Holy Spirit downloaded it to me.

It all begins with hearing. Think of it this way: a child will repeat whatever they hear. This is how we establish our ability to communicate with one another in speech. Proverbs 18:21 says that *"Death and life are in the power of the tongue."* Our tongue gives us the ability to create the atmosphere around us—an aroma which influences everyone we meet.

We often use essential oils in our home. We diffuse them into the atmosphere, and the scents of those oils provide us with certain soothing feelings. They change the mood or the atmosphere in our home.

If a stomach bug invades our space, we have an oil to shut it down. If we need to have a stressful conversation, I can use a certain oil to produce a calm serenity in the room. The scent that is produced in the atmosphere shifts how and what we are feeling. In the same way, we can use our words to shift the atmosphere around us.

Most of us would say that, at one time or another, we have gotten up in the middle of the night. Maybe we needed to get a drink of water, maybe we needed to use the restroom, or maybe we needed to check on our children. When I am in my own home, I don't worry about turning on the light because I know the location of each piece of furniture. We are comfortable walking in dark places as long as we know the lay of the land. It is when we are treading new territory that this becomes a problem.

When we rely on "feeling our way through" a space, we may end up with bruised legs and stubbed toes. It would have been much easier had we just turned on the light. Right?

The application of this in the spirit realm is that we have a guide who will help us when we cannot see. Jeremiah 33:3 says, *"Call to Me, and I will answer you, and show you great and mighty things, which you do not know."*

This is the beauty of faith: believing and trusting in the unseen hand of God. This belief comes first by developing the ability to hear from the Spirit of God. The full benefit of having a guide is listening to what the guide says and following the path the guide gives us!

PREPARE YOUR WEAPON

We have been given a powerful weapon against the enemy. It is our ability to speak. The other senses are important, but this one has to be manifested by our will in order to produce results. In other words, this weapon will not work unless we use it—we have to speak!

NEXT

One of my spiritual mothers said it best, "Your life will follow your words." That is the absolute truth. The difference between stopping or advancing in life can be summed up in one of two options: we are either *creating* mountains by speaking *about* them, or we are *moving* mountains by speaking *to* them.

"For assuredly, I say to you, whoever says to this mountain, 'Be removed and be cast into the sea,' and does not doubt in his heart, but believes that those things he says will be done, he will have whatever he says" (Mark 11:23).

When we get to the place in life that we are tired of the limitations placed on us by the enemy or by adverse circumstances, we will achieve a boldness in the spirit to change the environment around us—regardless of man's opinion. We need to get bold and declare "Mountain, get out of my way!"

Let's look at a passage in the Bible about a man who decided to live beyond what society labeled him to be. He heard that Jesus was coming to town. Surely, if his circumstances were ever going to change, it would be now.

Now they came to Jericho. As He went out of Jericho with His disciples and a great multitude, blind Bartimaeus, the son of Timaeus, sat by the road begging. And when he heard that it was Jesus of Nazareth, he began to cry out and say, "Jesus, Son of David, have mercy on me!"

Then many warned him to be quiet; but he cried out all the more, "Son of David, have mercy on me!" So Jesus stood still and commanded him to be called.

Then they called the blind man, saying to him, "Be of good cheer. Rise, He is calling you." And throwing aside his garment, he rose and came to Jesus. So Jesus answered and said to him, "What do you want Me to do for you?" The blind man said to Him, "Rabboni, that I may receive my sight." Then Jesus said to him, "Go your way; your faith has made you well." And immediately he received his sight and followed Jesus on the road.

Mark 10:46-52

I feel that we all can relate to this man in some way. Maybe we have been blinded before, physically or spiritually. Maybe we have had others around us who attempted to keep us in that condition because they didn't understand that there was a power that could get us out.

The first verse in this passage reads like this: "And they came to Jericho."

Following that, it says; "As He went out of Jericho..." What is the relevance of these two lines? Why would it say they *came to* and they *went out*? Consider the old city of Jericho.

This was the city of promise, surrounded by walls that God supernaturally brought down, and given into the hands of the Israelites. Before the walls fell down, no one went out and no one came in. Joshua 6:1 says, *"Now Jericho was securely shut up because of the children of Israel; none went out, and none came in."*

Jesus may have walked into Jericho and then walked out just to prove that He could. A city that had once been shut up had been liberated by a shout. Sometimes we just need to be reminded of the freedom which we have been given. Old mindsets are hard to break. When God is trying to get us to move past the old and step into the new, there will always be people there to remind us of how limited we really are.

Blind Bartimaeus heard that Jesus was coming. He couldn't see Him yet, but he heard Him. Can you imagine the chatter in the streets that day?

"Jesus is here! Have you heard about Him? Did you hear about the time He spit in the mud, rubbed it in the eyes of a man, told him to wash in the pool of Siloam, and he regained his sight?"

I wasn't there that day, but I am guessing this story struck a special chord with blind Bartimaeus. This story must have been the one that pushed him past the point of caring what others thought about him.

The old mindset of Jericho was still lingering. A city that once was shut up still had a mindset of being "shut up." Many warned Bartimaeus to "be quiet," as if he were disrupting things and drawing attention to himself. They may have been embarrassed by his outburst. However, the scripture says that this made him even more determined to cry out to Jesus.

Jesus, Son of David, have mercy on me!

It is likely that he remembered hearing the stories that had been passed down from previous generations: the walls of Jericho had been brought down by a victorious SHOUT.

If I push past the noise of the crowd and the spirit of "be quiet," Jesus will hear me and remove my walls of limitations.

We know that Jesus did just that. He heard this man's desperate plea, and it stopped Him in His tracks. Just like I know the cry of my child, God knows the cry of His. He knows when we are whining, and He knows when we are desperate. Our voice produces a sound like no one else's on this earth.

YOUR VOICE IS A WEAPON

Our visit to the zoo and our encounter with the snake had a profound impact on me. In the days following, all I could think of was that the enemy could not hear my words, but he could feel my vibrations. I could sense the Holy Spirit prompting me to research what happens when we speak.

I learned that when we speak, air passing through the larynx causes the vocal cords to vibrate which, in turn, produces our special sound.

This puzzled me. How could the enemy hang around those who murmur, complain or speak with hate, if the vibrations of the vocal cords scare a serpent? I've seen anger arise and be louder than the voice of excitement.

In my research, I found that our vocal cords are affected by our emotions. Stress, worry, fear, sadness, and anxiety can all change the sound that our vocal cords produce.

There is a humming of certain vibrations that is soothing to the adversary of our soul. He knows that if we are engaged in making these sounds, we will not be speaking the Word and exerting our authority over him. We must ask the Lord for discernment to divide emotion from spirit. Know the spirit that is in operation.

Have you ever left a conversation and felt like you needed a bath, like you needed to feel clean? The enemy loves bringing condemnation and filth. His goal is to muddy the waters and cause a stench to come into the atmosphere.

NEXT

My purpose in this moment is to remind you who you are in Christ, to commission you not to be intimidated, but to push back against the very tactic that is brought against you. However, keep it under the right authority and the right spirit. Second Corinthians 3:17 says, *"Now the Lord is the Spirit; and where the Spirit of the Lord is, there is liberty."*

There is a certain sound that terrifies the enemy, a certain sound that he cannot hang around. When we begin to speak in faith to the mountain that is set before us, it has to move. More than that, when we lift up our voice as a weapon of praise to God, the enemy cannot stand any longer. It truly places a dividing line between us and our

> **Lift Your Voice As a Weapon of Praise to God**

enemy and sets the course of what our NEXT looks like. The enemy cannot remain where the Spirit of the Lord is lifted high.

That is one of the reasons we spend time in church worshiping God together. Our worship leaders aren't trying to pump us up just to make noise, but they're trying to teach us how to run the devil out of our house when we get back home. They are showing us how to see victory in our lives.

How we respond in the heat of the battle determines our outcome. When we are faced with difficult circumstances, we can praise God for the outcome we need. We can start by saying the following:

- I trust you, Lord.
- I know You are *for* me.
- This is not my battle.
- You are the only One worthy of glory.

We can shift the atmosphere with our worship. We can speak words of faith and defeat the enemy. We can wear the full armor of God. Ephesians 6:10-17 says:

Finally, my brethren, be strong in the Lord and in the power of His might. Put on the whole armor of God, that you may be able to stand against the wiles of the devil. For we do not wrestle against flesh and blood, but against principalities, against powers, against the rulers of the darkness of this age, against spiritual hosts of wickedness in the heavenly places. Therefore take up the whole armor of God, that you may be able to withstand in the evil day, and having done all, to stand. Stand therefore, having girded your waist with truth, having put on the breastplate of righteousness, and having shod your feet with the preparation of the gospel of peace; above all, taking the shield of faith with which you will be able to quench all the fiery darts of the wicked one. And take the helmet of salvation, and the sword of the Spirit, which is the word of God.

People of God, rise up and take the authority that has been given to you. God wants you to be able to hear His voice above ALL the lies of the enemy.

Hear the truth of God, speak the truth of God, and see all that He has done for you in your *now*. Speak His truth. Don't mistake emotion for truth. His truth will set you and everyone around you free. Don't allow the enemy to steal one more second of your *now*, because your *now* is the pathway to your NEXT.

Chapter Seven

CAVE MOMENTS

And there he went into a cave, and spent the night in that place; and behold, the word of the LORD came to him, and He said to him, "What are you doing here, Elijah?"

1 Kings 19:9

FROM THE DESK OF AARON:

A few weeks before Easter Sunday 2018, the church renovated the sanctuary to make room for more people to attend. The church was growing at a rapid pace, and we were beginning to run out of space. We started this process by cutting off the front of the stage to free up more space and give it a fresh look.

The staff and many volunteers pitched in to accomplish this task. Excitement was in the air. Even though there was such a movement of growth, I was feeling a dryness in my spirit. I had felt this feeling before, but I had never experienced anything like this or to this magnitude.

On Easter Sunday, we had record-breaking attendance. Worship was incredible as always, but as soon as I stepped into the pulpit, I felt as though God's presence had lifted from me. I knew God was still moving among the congregation, but personally, I felt like I was searching for

God's touch concerning my calling. Despite the presence of God that was manifested in the service, I felt like I was in a dry place. The feeling was so strange.

Weeks later, we were attending *Stronger*, a women's conference hosted by Kathy Crabb Hannah. A woman came up to Amanda and me and began to speak over our lives. She said, "You will be ministering from a dry place in the next six months."

Her words stopped me in my tracks because Amanda was the only person who knew what I had been experiencing. The crazy thing is that this woman had no clue that on a Wednesday night in January, I had declared from the platform that in six months things would look totally different. I knew instantly that she was talking about the word I had spoken. God will always use a prophetic voice to confirm what you feel in your spirit, whether it comes through a vessel or through His written Word.

A Prophetic Voice

The renovations in our sanctuary marked the beginning of the visible changes, but I knew that God wanted to do something internally for our NEXT.

As this woman of God continued to speak, she said, "You will go through this season, but when you get to the other side of it, you two will step into an apostolic anointing! And when you preach about the river that's coming, everyone will know that something is different."

She continued by saying, "You are builders, and you were sent to Hendersonville by God because there is a fresh anointing flowing, and God is about to do more."

I am learning that when God fills His people with new wine, the structure will change. Mark 2:22 says, *"… no one puts new wine into old wineskins; or else the new wine bursts the wineskins, the wine is spilled, and the wineskins are ruined. But new wine must be put into new wineskins."*

The old way of doing things cannot support the fresh move of God. Joel 2:28-29 speaks of an end-time outpouring of the Holy Spirit:

> *And it shall come to pass afterward that I will pour out My Spirit on all flesh; your sons and your daughters shall prophesy, your old men shall dream dreams, your young men shall see visions. And also on My menservants and on My maidservants I will pour out My Spirit in those days.*

This passage is not speaking of just one event, but of a time—*those days*—when God's Spirit will be poured out in abundance on all who will receive it. When these outpourings come, the present wineskins will tear; they will not be able to sustain the new wine. There will be a shaking of the Church, the leaders, and the structures. As we are looking for a move of God—our NEXT—we must be looking for a new wineskin.

The woman continued speaking to us, declaring that there were many church plants in our future, and that God was preparing and positioning us for the harvest and for a fresh outpouring of His Spirit. This was all confirmation of what God had previously told us.

NEXT

I learned through the dry place—a cave moment, if you will— to hear God more clearly than ever before, much like the moment Elijah experienced in the shelter of the rock.

We find Elijah, the mighty prophet of God, hiding in a cave. We find out why in 1 Kings 19:1-4:

> *And Ahab told Jezebel all that Elijah had done, also how he had executed all the prophets with the sword. Then Jezebel sent a messenger to Elijah, saying, "So let the gods do to me, and more also, if I do not make your life as the life of one of them by tomorrow about this time." And when he saw that, he arose and ran for his life, and went to Beersheba, which belongs to Judah, and left his servant there.*
>
> *But he himself went a day's journey into the wilderness, and came and sat down under a broom tree. And he prayed that he might die, and said, "It is enough! Now, LORD, take my life, for I am no better than my fathers!"*

Elijah goes from prophesying on the mountain top to praying he might die under the juniper tree. When he arrived at the tree, he was exhausted, depressed, and ready to die. After he spent the night in the cave, God said to him, "What are you doing here?" Elijah thought he had come there to die; God knew he had come there to be revived!

GOD HAD A PLAN

God had a plan for this moment of his life. This tree provided renewal. The scent of the tree's white blossoms soothed his senses, and the softness of the petals as they covered the ground beneath him gave him a comfortable place to rest. The tree represented renewal, restoration, and a fresh vigor. What had faded was being made new.

Just as we can see God renewing Elijah using the properties of this tree, we know that He renews us through the sacrifice of Christ on another tree—the tree, the burial, and the resurrection.

Isaiah 40:31 says, *But those who wait on the LORD shall renew their strength; They shall mount up with wings as eagles, They shall run and not grow weary, They shall walk and not faint.* The waiting part is difficult, but God is always working in the waiting. In Christ, we find rest and strength, restoration and resurrection.

After Elijah had rested a while under the tree, an angel appeared with food and drink for him. This meal gave him strength for the next 40 days as he made his way to Mount Horeb, where he took refuge in a cave. Elijah's time in the cave is symbolic of the refuge that you and I can find in God. Elijah's refuge was a cave; our refuge is Christ. As long as we are found *"in Christ,"* we have nothing to fear.

Some scholars believe that since this cave was located on Mount Horeb, it could very well have been *"the cleft of the rock"* where God placed Moses when His glory passed by (Exodus 33:21-23). It is here that we see Elijah, hiding in a cave cowering in anxiety, fearing for his life.

Elijah was running for his life because Ahab, the wicked King of Israel, had told Queen Jezebel what Elijah had done—slaying the false prophets of Baal and calling down fire from heaven. Jezebel sent a messenger to Elijah and said, "I'm going to kill you."

NEXT

Jezebel's words had sketched such a picture in Elijah's mind, and gripped his heart so tightly in panic and dread that he *"arose and ran for his life."* (1 Kings 19:3).

He went from the mountaintop to the broom tree, and now from the broom tree to a dark place of hiding.

Do Not Be Driven by Fear

Just as faith comes by hearing and hearing by the Word of God, fear comes by hearing and hearing by the words of the world. Fear had driven Elijah right into a place of emptiness, loneliness, and depression. He needed to find a place where he could find strength in his body, his mind, and his attitude.

There are so many reasons that we can find ourselves in this kind of situation: divorce, abuse, the cares of the ministry, or a broken heart. If a mighty man of God such as Elijah can experience a cave moment, so can we. If it happened to him, there are others who'll experience it, too.

Even King David took refuge in a cave while hiding from Saul: *"David therefore departed from there and escaped to the cave of Adullam…"* (1 Samuel 22:1). Consider Obadiah. He hid 100 of the Lord's prophets in a cave. There, they were sustained and saved from the hand of Jezebel, whose plan was to destroy every prophet of God in the land. Hiding in the cave saved them from certain destruction (1 Kings 18:4).

I am sure hiding in the cave did not seem reasonable. Kings and prophets are not the kind of people who hide. Kings are looked upon as fearless leaders, and prophets are considered the bold ones, fearlessly proclaiming the Word of the Lord among the people.

A cave may be a place of fear; it is cold, musty and undesirable. It is dark and uninviting. But a cave might just be the safest place to be. It might be the only place we can hear from God. In the cave, we are alone. We are protected, hidden away from all the distractions of life. Away from all the competing voices in our lives, God's voice can become crystal clear.

Elijah spent a long, dark night in the cave. The next day, he heard the voice of God saying, "What are you doing here, Elijah?" Some of us know what it feels like to be in a cave. We come to the mountain of God where it seems like glory should be all around, where there should be unspeakable joy, and where we should be enveloped in the presence of God. Instead, it feels like God is a million miles away. But let me reassure you, something always happens NEXT.

It might seem like everyone around us is partaking of the blessings from Heaven, but we can't feel anything. We are at a place of questioning our experience, our calling, and whether we are really anointed at all. *Did we miss God somewhere?*

The enemy is a liar. We are facing what Elijah faced: we are in the cave. No, we are not backslidden, we haven't disobeyed God, and he hasn't forsaken us. We are still called; we are still anointed. We are in a *hiding-out* season.

God has not changed his mind about using us. This cave moment is temporary, and we are coming out of this. The cave was exactly what Elijah needed at this period of his life. The cave is a place of dread; it is dark, lonely, and confining, but I am convinced that the cave is critical. When we find ourselves in a cave, we are in the process of growth.

The cave can be a tomb if we allow it to be, but it can also be a place of resurrection. We can either die or progress. Our ministry can be birthed afresh and anew—if we can handle the cave moment.

Our first tendency is to resist it and fight against it. Many times, we try to keep going—trudging forward and pretending like everything is good—until we can't pretend anymore. Then, we just quit.

Look at the cave from a different perspective. Look at it as a birthing place and a place of restoration. Look at the cave as a place of refuge and resurrection.

I know what the cave through natural eyes represents: darkness, no vision. We can't see where we are going. When we lose vision, we lose purpose, and losing our sense of purpose will kill our passion. But be encouraged: allow the tomb to become a place where dead things live again.

The cave is the place where we are compelled to stop. It is the place where we are left alone to contend with God. It is the place where we are forced to examine ourselves and to take inventory. It is the place where we answer the question: *What are we doing here?* Are we moving with the anointing, or are we just going through the motions? Are we operating on a word from God? Have we lost the vision?

If we will respond correctly to the dark place, it will become a resting place—a womb of fresh perception, divine revelation, and a fresh anointing. We will come out with a renewed sense of purpose and an unquenchable passion, with a power as never before. After God questioned Elijah, He began to speak to

Be Sure to Respond Correctly

him about his future. What looked like the end of Elijah's life became the launching pad for the NEXT phase of his ministry. His setback was a setup for His comeback. We can't afford to become so overpowered with what has happened in the past that we can't see what God is doing right in front of us.

What launched Elijah from his cave and into the final phase of his ministry was a word from the Lord. When the word of the Lord came to Elijah, it carried a new vision, a new sense of purpose, and a new passion. Elijah left that cave with a fresh pep in his step and a great anointing. He was no longer looking back, but ahead and carrying the anointing to the next generation. One word from God had turned his tomb into a womb and his ministry was reborn. He was a man on fire—fueled by a renewed sense of purpose.

TOUCH NOT GOD'S ANOINTED

When David hid from Saul in the cave of Adullam, it just so happened that Saul decided to rest in the very same cave! (1 Samuel 24:3). Saul did not realize that David and his men were there, hiding in the recesses of the cave.

It was here that David's men encouraged him to take Saul out, but David wouldn't put a hand against him. He said to his men, *"The LORD forbid that I should do this thing to my master, the LORD's anointed"* (1 Samuel 24:6).

Here, in the same cave, were two anointings. There was Saul, yesterday's king with yesterday's anointing. Saul had been used of God to do great things, but he failed to make the shift. Then there was David, tomorrow's king with tomorrow's anointing. David represented transition—a fresh new beginning, a hope and a future.

In every cave, there are two anointings: the old and the new. Which one will come out of our cave experience? Resignation or transformation? Will we *realign* or *resign*?

We can't live the rest of our life looking back, talking about how it used to be, what God used to do, and how God used to move. I'm not saying that the old was bad, but it was time to change. Elijah had a great anointing, but when it was time to change, the cave became that place of transformation. When Elijah left that cave, he was renewed, and fearless.

I declare that a fearless anointing will follow us out of whatever cave we find ourselves in. I declare that aggressive faith will consume us, and that Jezebel spirit will bother us no more.

Nothing changed *outside* the cave. Jezebel did not change, nor did Ahab. For any change to occur, Elijah had to go *inside* the cave.

Just as a caterpillar could never transition into a beautiful multi-colored butterfly without the process of the dark cocoon, you and I cannot make the transition to a new and fresh anointing without a cave.

Whatever drives us into the cave will open the way for us to hear from God about our future. We are about to come out dripping in oil, and the very thing that ran us into the cave will be responsible for pushing us into our NEXT.

Chapter Eight

RECALL

FROM THE DESK OF AMANDA:

"Abraham!" There was a weight of authority in God's voice as He called Abraham's name.

"Here I am."

"I want you to go to the land of Moriah and take Isaac, your only son, and offer him there as a burnt offering."

The story of Abraham and Isaac is one of great faith and great obedience. God had promised to make him the father of many nations, but he and his wife Sarah had no children. When Abraham was 99 years old, God told them they would have a son—a son through whom God's promise to Abraham would come to pass. Even though they laughed to think that such a thing was still possible, a year later, Sarah bore a son they named Isaac, which meant "laughter."

Isaac was just a young boy when God tested Abraham by telling him to take his son and offer him as a burnt sacrifice. Though filled with sadness and grief, Abraham prepared for the journey to Moriah. Without hesitation, he gathered up the necessary supplies and set off for the mountains with Isaac.

Although he did not understand why he was being asked to sacrifice his son, Abraham had complete faith in God. He didn't know how it would happen, but he knew that God would provide an answer.

When Isaac saw all the preparations for a sacrifice, he asked his father, "Where is the lamb?" Abraham's reply reverberates through history: *God will provide Himself a lamb.*

When they reached the mountain, Abraham laid the wood and prepared the fire. He tied up Isaac and lifted his hand to slay him. At that moment, the angel of the Lord stopped him and said, "Do not lay a hand on the boy. Do not harm him. Now I know that you fear God: you were willing to sacrifice your son."

Abraham stopped, looked up, and saw a ram caught in a thicket. Together, Abraham and Isaac made the altar ready and sacrificed the ram that God had provided. Abraham named the place Jehovah-Jireh, which means "the Lord provides."

Here is the biblical account found in Genesis 22:1-19:
Now it came to pass after these things that God tested Abraham, and said to him, "Abraham!"
And he said, "Here I am."
Then He said, "Take now your son, your only son Isaac, whom you love, and go to the land of Moriah, and offer him there as a burnt offering on one of the mountains of which I shall tell you."
So Abraham rose early in the morning and saddled his donkey, and took two of his young men with him, and

Isaac his son; and he split the wood for the burnt offering, and arose and went to the place of which God had told him. Then on the third day Abraham lifted his eyes and saw the place afar off. And Abraham said to his young men, "Stay here with the donkey; the lad and I will go yonder and worship, and we will come back to you."

So Abraham took the wood of the burnt offering and laid it on Isaac his son; and he took the fire in his hand, and a knife, and the two of them went together. But Isaac spoke to Abraham his father and said, "My father!"

And he said, "Here I am, my son."

Then he said, "Look, the fire and the wood, but where is the lamb for a burnt offering?"

And Abraham said, "My son, God will provide for Himself the lamb for a burnt offering." So the two of them went together.

Then they came to the place of which God had told him. And Abraham built an altar there and placed the wood in order; and he bound Isaac his son and laid him on the altar, upon the wood. And Abraham stretched out his hand and took the knife to slay his son.

But the Angel of the LORD called to him from heaven and said, "Abraham, Abraham!"

So he said, "Here I am."

And He said, "Do not lay your hand on the lad, or do anything to him; for now I know that you fear God, since you have not withheld your son, your only son, from Me."

Then Abraham lifted his eyes and looked, and there behind him was a ram caught in a thicket by its horns. So Abraham went and took the ram, and offered it up for a

burnt offering instead of his son. And Abraham called the name of the place, The-LORD-Will-Provide; as it is said to this day, "In the Mount of the LORD it shall be provided."
Then the Angel of the LORD called to Abraham a second time out of heaven, and said: "By Myself I have sworn, says the LORD, because you have done this thing, and have not withheld your son, your only son— blessing I will bless you, and multiplying I will multiply your descendants as the stars of the heaven and as the sand which is on the seashore; and your descendants shall possess the gate of their enemies.
In your seed all the nations of the earth shall be blessed, because you have obeyed My voice." So Abraham returned to his young men, and they rose and went together to Beersheba; and Abraham dwelt at Beersheba.

ABRAHAM'S FAITH CONFIRMED

Has God ever asked you to do something difficult? Has He ever required you to give him something that is precious to you?

We want to paint the picture that God would never require something difficult from us. He would never want us to suffer or feel any type of pain or loss. While pain and loss are not in God's plan for us, He will, at times, test our faith. Is our trust fully in Him, or do we place more trust in all the blessings He has given us?

Pastor Aaron and I have been on an incredible journey as you can tell by the stories within the pages of this book, but these words didn't come without a price. There were times God asked us to bring an Isaac up the mountain, to see if we would move, regardless of what it looked like.

We, being human, cannot fathom why God would ask such a thing. Why would He ask us to give up something that is a promise or a blessing to our household? The message is simple—God wants to know the level of trust we have in Him. He wants to know if He can take us into our NEXT.

In verse 16, the Lord said to Abraham, *"Because you have done this thing, I will bless you and multiply your seed as the stars in heaven."* There was a great exchange that took place. God was saying to Abraham, "I now know, that no matter what I give you, it will never take my place in your heart."

God desires to release the bigger blessing to us, but we can't let go of what we currently have, for fear that we will be left with nothing.

A perfect example of this is in tithes and offerings. Sadly, many of us do not have a clear understanding about why we are giving. Our human minds want to see where our money is going, instead of simply walking by faith and releasing it into the kingdom of God. Does God need our money? No. Did God need Abraham's son? No. However, God will test us to see where our heart is. Matthew 6:21 says, *"For where your treasure is, there your heart will be also."*

Whatever we struggle the most to let go of is often the thing that controls us. Aaron and I have had our fair share of struggles in life. We know what it is like to have abundance, and we know what it is like to nearly lose everything. Yet God was, and is, still God.

NEXT

In one of our seasons of struggle, Aaron and I were attending a conference. I had been invited to minister at the conference and had received an honorarium. I was holding the check in my hand, calculating how much the tithe would be on it. I held the check up to the heavens, and I prayed: *Thank You for Your blessing. You know it has been a season of struggle, and You know how much we need this. Thank You for always providing for us; even if it is late, it is still in Your perfect time.*

| He Is Jehovah Jireh |

As I was writing the tithe check out, I heard the Lord say, "Give it all to me."

What? Lord, You know where we are. You know how badly we need this!

I heard Him speak so clearly, "Is this your source? If it is, I will let you keep it. But if you will release it to me, watch and see what I will do!"

I stopped writing the tithe check and slipped into the auditorium where another service was now in progress. Check in hand, I sat down next to Aaron. I whispered in his ear what the Lord had spoken to me. I waited for him to tell me that I had incorrectly heard from the Lord, but that wasn't what he said. He responded by saying, "Amanda, I trust that the Holy Spirit has spoken this to you."

This wasn't just a small amount; this was one month's pay, and there weren't any other conference bookings on the calendar. I gripped that check in my hand, and I said to the Lord, "I want you more than anything. You are my source." Then, I released it. I wanted the earth to quake, the lightning to strike or a choir of angels to sing. Instead, I heard the still, small voice of the Holy Spirit leading me to Isaiah 60:5:

Then you shall see and become radiant, And your heart shall swell with joy; Because the abundance of the sea shall be turned to you, The wealth of the Gentiles shall come to you.

As I read verse 5, I knew I was entering into a place I had never ever experienced before—a new place of trust in Him that couldn't be learned any other way. He was enlarging my heart because the abundance of the sea would be turning toward us. If my heart were to remain in a small space toward Him, then the abundance that was approaching would overwhelm and overtake me like a wave crashing onto the shore.

Over the next few weeks, God supernaturally provided in ways that I did not see coming. He truly caused the ravens to come and feed us when our stream appeared to be almost dried up. I told God, "This doesn't look like a wave—this looks like a trickle." He reminded me that a trickle is still movement, and it is still provision.

About three months passed, and the Lord spoke to me about an amount that was coming all at once. I didn't see how that much money could be coming, but that didn't cause me to have disbelief. I trusted even when I didn't see it: *God will provide Himself a lamb.*

GOD WILL ALWAYS BE OUR TRUE SOURCE

Sometimes we need to recall the word of the Lord to us. God had asked me the question: "Can I be your source?" He wasn't telling me that He *would be* my source; He was asking me if He *could be* my source. It had to be a confession and exchange on my end: if I believed that He was my source, I also believed that He would do everything He had promised, and then some.

After three months of trusting without being moved by fear, the Lord showed Himself mightily. He supernaturally placed in our hands four times the amount that I had sown. I did not sow it to get more, I gave it to Him because He asked me for it. When He asks us for something, He has a purpose in mind. He intends to not only replenish that which was sacrificed, but to multiply it as well.

Money is a language that we all speak. It is the currency that we need in order to live in the natural world. There are many promises in His Word that tell us that if we give, it will be given to us, *"pressed down, shaken together, and running over"* (Luke 6:38).

Since the beginning of our marriage, Aaron and I have been givers. That is often the very thing that the enemy will attempt to block. God doesn't need our money; He wants us to have faith and trust Him first. Satan doesn't need our money; he wants to steal our faith and cause us to trust in ourselves. He always works to counter what God speaks.

Abraham trusted the Lord, but he found himself creating a false promise. How many times have we done that in life? We don't see God moving when we think He should, so *we* decide how and when God should move. As a result, an Ishmael is born, and trouble enters the camp.

We might look at this story and think: *how could a father love one son more than the other? How could Abraham send one to the desert away from him but allow the other to remain?*

When Abraham sent Hagar and Ishmael out of the camp, it wasn't just for the sake of Sarah. It was more about removing the false idols—the self-created answer to prayer—out of the camp. The fact that Abraham would take Isaac, the promised son, up the mountain to obey the voice of God proves he would do whatever the Lord asked of him.

Abraham's spiritual hearing was being tested. By conceiving Ishmael, Abraham had already tried to fulfill God's promise himself by listening to the words of others around him. Now, God wanted to know if Abraham could hear Him clearly by giving him this instruction to take Isaac up the mountain alone.

We have been in a season of laying things down. In past seasons, we made many decisions based on the flesh instead of the Spirit. Even though we could easily justify how the things we were doing would help further the kingdom work of God, we often found ourselves wishing that we had listened to that inner voice instead. It doesn't mean these things would not be right for others, but they weren't right for us.

One of the decisions we made was to buy a bus. We felt that this had to be the way God intended for us to travel and minister as a family. Because we had not listened to God, we spent many nights broken down along deserted highways. It ended up costing us more in both time and money than it should have because it was out of the will of God for us.

NEXT

We tend to think that a "no" from God means we will be left out or left behind or lacking in some way. But the reality is that God knows the future, and we don't. He knew that our season of travel would be short-lived. He knew that we would soon be positioned in one of the largest churches in America where we would be leading worship and would have no need of a bus. He also knew that a recession was about to hit, and no one else would want that bus, either. So, there we were, stuck with an Ishmael and asking God to make a way out for us. *The very mess He told us to avoid was the same mess we were now begging Him to clean up!*

> **God Knows What's Best; He Sees Our Future**

How thankful we are that God isn't limited to our ignorance! How many times could we have avoided what we knew was the wrong choice? I have to believe that Abraham had that knowing inside. Although he loved Ishmael, he knew that this child wasn't the child of promise. He had become an idol.

Abraham had come from a bloodline of people who worshiped idols. God had told him, "Leave your family and all of their idol worship and go to the place I will show you." He had to remove the idols once before, and here he was, doing it again.

The day that he walked Isaac up the mountain was not the first day he had walked blindly, trusting God to lead and provide. Abraham had been in this place many times before. This time, there would be no substitute for the sacrifice. This time, there would be no false promise.

I have often thought, *What if I were Abraham?* Would I have been tempted to take a lamb up with me just in case God changed His mind about the mission? Would I have been looking for a safety net? We all have one—a Plan B to fall back on in case Plan A fails. However, Abraham said, "Not this time. There is NO Plan B. *God will provide Himself a lamb."*

We've had to remove the Plan B in our lives and simply trust that God will provide. We have had to let go of the mindset that if *this* doesn't work out, we can just fall back on *that.* We are living in a season of doubling down—it is all or nothing!

When God releases a promise to us, He doesn't intend for that to be the end of our relationship with Him, but rather a fresh point of beginning. He is the God of promise. He doesn't want us to receive one promise and stop trusting Him for more. When we start calling forth greater things, it requires an exchange from us. It may be time, money, resources, or familiar territory, but *something* has to give.

The story of Abraham shows us there is nothing new under the sun. Abraham was human, just like us. He struggled. Sarah struggled. Hagar struggled. Struggle is part of the human experience. Just like them, we want what we want when we want it. There are three enemies of God: the world, the flesh, and the devil.

The world says, "If it feels good, do it."

The flesh says, "I want it, and I want it now."

Then, there is Satan, the ruler of this dark age, who tells us the same thing he told Jesus: "Worship me, and I will give you everything!"

NEXT

We live in a society that is constantly telling us that if we get bored with one thing, we can just move on to the next. We don't value patience and perseverance, and we preach a message of all blessing and no sacrifice. Very seldom do we hear messages about knowing Jesus through the fellowship of His suffering (Philippians 3:10), or about taking up our cross and following Him (Matthew 16:24). However, the blessing and promise we have is that He will never leave nor forsake us, and He will be with us even to the end (Hebrews 13:5).

As we increased our giving this year, the warfare waged against us also increased. As we began to declare and see healing manifest in others, the enemy began to attack our own physical bodies, but we held onto the promises of God.

KEEP PRESSING FORWARD

In order to press forward toward the mark for the prize of the high calling of God (Philippians 3:14), we cannot hold on to what is behind. Reaching toward the future requires us to let go of the past. When God allows us to see a vision of the future, or speaks a prophetic word to us, it may take time to manifest. We can be certain, though, that if God has allowed us to see something or has spoken a specific word over us, that He will bring it to pass.

Often, we can see the beginning and the end of a thing, but God doesn't show us the middle. If He did, then chances are we wouldn't want to walk the journey. But, we can trust the process. We can confidently release what God has asked us to release. If we remain faithful to Him, we will see the end of our faith—we will enter into our NEXT.

God has a plan for us, and He wants us to make it all the way from His promise to His provision.

Are you going through a season where you feel hopeless and lost? Maybe you have never received a vision or a prophetic word from God that you can hold onto. If that is you, God has not left you without hope—you can hold onto the Word. The pages of God's Word are filled with promises just waiting to be discovered. The Word is enough—the Word is truth; His Word is truth. I've heard it said many times, "If you can't *hear* God, then *read* Him."

His word is Spirit-breathed, and we can receive from it every day. This is something I have learned that has led me to where I am today. I was the girl who was in church most of my life, but I had no revelation or understanding of who God really was. I had my own ideas about who God was and who God wanted me to be.

Jesus made it clear that if we've seen Him, we've seen the Father. If we want to know the way to the Father's heart, we must come through the blood of Jesus.

To create a life of hearing the voice of God, we must first become His sheep. He said in His Word, "*My sheep hear My voice*" (John 10:27). Sometimes, we read the Bible as if it were just another book, and we cannot do that. We must ask the Lord for understanding and revelation of what we are reading before we begin. Our prayer should be: *Give us this day our daily bread.* The same way we would find time to eat a healthy meal daily, we must have a diet of the Word to be able to hear and discern His voice clearly.

We often pride ourselves on knowledge, but we do not ask for understanding. Sadly, we often choose natural understanding over spiritual understanding. We want things to make sense to our flesh, and when they don't, we cast them off as being "not of God."

We don't have any record of Abraham questioning the Lord about the wisdom of bringing forth a son with Hagar. Abraham knew God's voice; but, in this situation, he allowed Sarah's desperation for a child to distract him. I believe this was the reason that he and Isaac had to go up the mountain alone. He couldn't allow another person's opinion to get in between him and God this time.

Fellowship and communion with the Lord lead to a trust that cannot be broken. When we don't just want the hand of God (the blessings), but we also want His heart, we will have a trust in Him that no circumstance can shake.

I pray that your heart will recall every promise that God has made to you. May you bring them back to the forefront of your spirit, and may you begin to breathe life into those promises. *God will provide Himself a lamb*. Abraham recalled God's promise in spite of his circumstances, and God took him into his NEXT.

> **Recall Every Promise**

Here is an exercise in faith that you can do: Write down three things God has promised you and put them where you can see them for the next 30 days. Speak over them as if they were already done and watch what God will do. If God's Word says it, God will do it. Mountains will move, wombs will be filled, marriages will be restored, and all the glory will go to God our Father! *God will provide Himself a lamb*, and He will surely lead us into our NEXT!

Chapter Nine

DIG

And Elisha said, "...bring me a musician." Then it happened, when the musician played, that the hand of the LORD came upon him. And he said, "Thus says the LORD: 'Make this valley full of ditches.' For thus says the LORD: 'You shall not see wind, nor shall you see rain; yet that valley shall be filled with water, so that you, your cattle, and your animals may drink....'
Now it happened in the morning, when the grain offering was offered, that suddenly water came by way of Edom, and the land was filled with water.

2 Kings 3:14-17, 20

FROM THE DESK OF AARON:

Three kings were in a desperate situation. They had been marching through the wilderness for seven days and had found no water. Their armies were suffering from thirst and their animals would not make it much longer.

King Jehoram of Israel had enlisted the help of King Jehoshaphat of Judah to go up against the king of Moab, who had rebelled against him. The king of Edom joined them as they crossed through his land on the way to Moab.

Three armies and all their animals filled the land, with no water in sight. Without water, they had no hope of victory. Without water, they would not survive.

The king of Israel was a wicked man, who *"did evil in the sight of God"* and had *"made Israel sin"* (2 Kings 3:2-3). He began to blame God for their situation; but Jehoshaphat, the godly king of Judah, knew the power of a word from God and the importance of the prophetic office.

"Is there no prophet of the LORD here, that we may inquire of the LORD by him? (v. 11). He knew that one word from God could change everything.

The three kings found the prophet Elisha, who did indeed have a word for them. It was more than just a word telling them that they would defeat their enemy; it was an instruction that would ensure their survival: *"Make this valley full of ditches"* (v. 16).

They were weak from lack of water and unsure of what was ahead, but they obeyed that word and began to dig ditches in the valley. In the morning, God sent water and filled the ditches to overflowing. They all had plenty of water and were able to gain strength to go on and defeat their enemy.

Being in a position to hear from God is crucial. Understanding the importance of an anointed word is invaluable. Obeying that word makes all the difference in our lives.

Sometimes God will give us a word we don't see coming. It might even be a word we don't want to hear, like "I know you are hot and thirsty, but start digging ditches in the valley." Such a word may not settle well when we find ourselves in the middle of a drought and in desperate need of water.

DEMANDING WORK

Digging ditches is demanding work. I used to work on a tree farm with my grandfather. My job was to help him cut down old trees, dig ditches, and fill them with the limbs and sticks from the old trees.

Then, we would dig holes to replace the old trees with new ones. Digging was especially difficult when the ground was hard and the land was dry.

Many days, we were a sweaty, dirty mess by the time we got home from working in the field. Our hands would be filthy, bloodied and blistered. But the work was done, and the trees we planted are still there today!

Why would God ask us to dig ditches in a dry and hard land? The answer is simple: so we will be ready to catch the water when it comes! If that is how God is speaking to us, it's time to roll up our sleeves and get to work.

We might look at this story and wonder how it could apply to us—after all, they were kings! But being a king could not save them from the lack of water. Being an elder or deacon in our church won't keep us from passing through a place of spiritual drought. We've all been in situations like this.

We've all had times when we have had to make ourselves pray, read our Bible, or go to church. We've all had periods when we've felt dry and empty. We've all gone through situations where it would have been easier to give up than to continue to dig those ditches. We've all

> **Keep Digging**

101

experienced seasons when we felt like our miracle was never going to happen.

We are never going to launch that ministry school; we're never going to complete that book; we're never going to start that business. We are never going to see our children saved; we are never going to get out of debt; we are never going to go minister to the nations. We are never going to reach our NEXT.

When we look at our present circumstances, it may seem like it's more than we can bear. But we have to make up our minds that we are going to hold on to our promise, no matter how it looks around us. We are going to hold on to our prophecy, our dream, and our vision—and just keep digging.

What do we do when we're standing in the dry and desolate place? Dig!

What do we do when there is a mountain standing in front of us? Dig!

What do we do when we find ourselves in the valley of the shadow of death? Dig!

The digging may require a great deal of work from us. It may be difficult at times, and it may not make much sense, but we need to keep digging. When we are in that low place where our hands are bleeding and our muscles are aching and we are covered in dirt, we need to keep digging.

There have been many moments like this in ministry for us. There have been times when the river was flowing, the blessings were coming, and the prophetic words were pouring out upon us. But then came the testing—the process before the promise, the season before the sight.

What showed up seemed to be the opposite of what God had declared. God had said we would enter a time of harvest, but it seemed we were losing more than we were reaping, like we were lacking more than we were releasing!

Then there was the time someone prophesied that *unity* in our church was going to cultivate a great move of God, but all hell broke loose, dividing people and trying to stop everything that had been spoken over us. What do we do? Dig!

We dig by reminding God of His Word (Isaiah 43:26). God promises us that if we search out His Word and speak it in faith, it will not return void (Isaiah 55:11).

When we dig, we are building a landing strip for God's blessings in our lives. Like the Israelites of old digging ditches in a dry valley, we are creating the capacity to receive the promise!

God's promise for us is a greater glory, a greater power, a greater anointing, and a greater blessing than we have ever had in our lives. The devil comes to steal, kill and destroy (John 10:10), but God's promise is that He will send the water of life into our lives at just the right moment.

Digging means that we keep on moving, keep on praying, keep on praising, keep on sowing, and keep on coming to church. We dig until moisture begins to flow into our circumstances.

GET READY FOR A HOLY GHOST DELUGE

Have you ever watched a road fill up with water during a summer rainstorm? Before the storm begins, there is the familiar smell of ozone in the air—a scent that tells us rain is coming. As the storm begins, the pavement is just dampened and darkened by the first drops of rain. Then, the drops get a little bigger and begin to splash up from the surface of the road. Finally, the rain comes down in such a downpour that it completely covers the roadway and overflows into the ditches and culverts along the sides of the road.

God is about to do something big. In the same way that the trees I planted with my grandfather eventually produced fruit, we will reap if we faint not. Due season is coming; our new season is coming. If we plant, we will also reap a harvest.

Digging means declaring that rain is heading our way, and the ditches we have been digging will be filled completely. The drought is over. A new season is on the way, and the drought will break in the very same valley where our enemy said we would die. Whether the valley is our ministry, our marriage, our health, or our finances, we will experience a brand-new supply of the glory and the power of God.

We can rise up with new boldness and new faith. We can rise up with new determination and new anointing. By faith, we can go to the enemy's camp and take back everything he stole from us during the season of drought.

There is a drought-breaking anointing in God's Word that has the ability to stir up our faith, if we can just smell the water:

For there is hope for a tree, If it is cut down, that it will sprout again, And that its tender shoots will not cease. Though its root may grow old in the earth, And its stump

*may die in the ground, Yet at the scent of water it will
bud, And bring forth branches like a plant.*

Job 14:7-9

Like a tree responding to the scent of water, hope will
grow again. At first, we may not be able to see it, but we can
sense the breakthrough, the miracle awakening in the air.
We may not see it yet, but by faith, we can catch the scent of
a new anointing. The atmosphere is changing. New life is
sprouting, and joy, restoration, and deliverance are being
released.

The devil will come against us and try to kill us in the
wilderness. He knows that if we can just get to the water
and tap into that hidden power, he will no longer have a
chance to stop us or destroy us. He thought we would never
last without water, but he never counted on us digging our
way back to life. He thought our situation would outlast us
and send us right back to Egypt.

I could have quit many times. I could have admitted
defeat and given up on my dream, but I had received a *word*.
I had received a word that my season was changing. I had
received a word that water was on the way. I had received
a word that said it was going to get better. I had received a
word from Psalm 30:5 that says, *"Weeping may endure for a
night, but joy comes in the morning."*

All Jehoshaphat needed was one word: *this valley shall be
filled with water.* Although we may not see it yet, water has
already been released from heaven—waters of joy and
rivers of vision. There is an undercurrent flowing; there is a
rumbling in the spirit; there is about to be a breakthrough.

NEXT

We are right on the edge of our miracle. The drought is breaking, our season is changing, and our spiritual drought is over! The scent of water is in the air.

Now is not the time to stop digging. If we can find the strength to fill one more shovel full of dirt, the heavens will open, and the rain will be released. If we can lift one more *Hallelujah* to the Lord, the atmosphere around us will begin to change. If we can march around those walls one more time, the walls of debt will fall down around us.

Our marriages will be restored, our sicknesses will be healed, and our children will be saved. Our valley will be full of ditches that are overflowing with water.

God will not send the water just because we are thirsty, or just because we are dry, or just because we're in trouble. God loves us, and He wants to meet our needs exceedingly and abundantly. God not only wants to meet our needs and deliver us; He wants us to be so filled up with passion and power that the enemy will be sorry he ever bothered us.

After Elisha gave the three kings the instructions from the Lord to fill the valley with ditches, he followed it up with a promise: their enemy would be delivered into their hands and would be totally and completely defeated:

> *And this is a simple matter in the sight of the LORD; He will also deliver the Moabites into your hand. Also you shall attack every fortified city and every choice city, and shall cut down every good tree, and stop up every spring of water, and ruin every good piece of land with stones.*

> 2 Kings 3:18-19

It happened for the three kings who went to war together, and it will happen for us. Not only will our valleys be filled with water, we will go into our enemy's camp, stop up his wells, ruin his land, and emerge victorious.

Our future is secure; we will not die in the wilderness. Our valley will be filled with water, and we will invade the enemy's camp and take back *everything* he has stolen from us. This is our NEXT!

Conclusion

TRANSITIONING THROUGH TRIALS

For all things are for your sakes, that grace, having spread through the many, may cause thanksgiving to abound to the glory of God.

Therefore we do not lose heart. Even though our outward man is perishing, yet the inward man is being renewed day by day. For our light affliction, which is but for a moment, is working for us a far more exceeding and eternal weight of glory, while we do not look at the things which are seen, but at the things which are not seen. For the things which are seen are temporary, but the things which are not seen are eternal.

2 Corinthians 4:15-18

FROM THE DESK OF AARON:

T he children of Israel had just been released from their captivity by Pharaoh. God told Moses that the people were to camp at Pi Hahiroth, between the town of Migdol and the Red Sea. There was only one problem with this location: Pharaoh had changed his mind about letting the children of Israel go, and he had sent his army in pursuit.

With the Egyptian army behind them and the Red Sea in front of them, they had nowhere left to go. God had not only allowed them to be in this position, He had orchestrated it Himself! God knew the plans and purposes He had for the children of Israel, and He knew the plan He had for their escape. The sea opened and allowed them to cross; it closed again on the pursuing army.

There was an *"exceeding and eternal weight of glory"* at work in this situation. God's name would be honored among the Egyptians, and God's people would be preserved to bring forth the Messiah in their future.

I have learned from my own life that God will sometimes allow us to get into a place where our back is against the wall. He will allow us to stand before a Red Sea with an Egyptian army closing in on us. He will let us go through a fiery furnace. He will let us spend the night in a hungry den of lions. Why?

It is a test of our faith. It is a test to see what is in our hearts. In Deuteronomy 8:16, like the Israelites, we are reminded that it was God *"who fed you in the wilderness with manna, which your fathers did not know, that He might humble you and that He might test you, to do you good in the end."*

According to 2 Corinthians 4, these things are temporary. They are the things that are seen. The things that are not seen are eternal. The Bible calls them a *"light affliction, which is but for a moment, ... working for us a far more exceeding and eternal weight of glory."* Our afflictions are producing His glory, accomplishing His purposes in our lives.

The glory is way out of proportion to the affliction. The trial that seems so *heavy* to us is *light* in comparison to the eternal weight of glory that God wants to release upon us.

Even though life has challenging seasons for us to walk through, there is a NEXT for us. What we are going through is not forever. Our temporary problem that seems so massive to us becomes small in comparison to our eternal promise from God whose assurance in Isaiah 61:3 is:

> *To console those who mourn in Zion, To give them beauty for ashes, The oil of joy for mourning, The garment of praise for the spirit of heaviness; That they may be called trees of righteousness, The planting of the LORD, that He may be glorified.*

THE DESERT MENTALITY

As a pastor of new church plant, I had those moments when I was worried! I had never done this before. There were moments when I was afraid that I would do the wrong things or say the wrong things.

One Sunday morning I was so burdened about a situation—so taken up with thinking about the problems and wondering what to do—that I didn't even know where I was. I felt inadequate to deal with the issues, but I began to pray this prayer of commitment to the Lord: *Lord, please forgive me. I know better than this. I know better than to worry. I shouldn't be this overly concerned about anything.*

In that moment, I heard the Holy Spirit reminding me to cast all my cares on Him (1 Peter 5:7).

I continued praying: *Lord, I turn it all over to you. I'm not going to worry anymore about what I can't fix. You sent me here to plant this church. I will preach Your Word. I will walk in love and treat others according to Your Word. I'll lay hands on*

Continue Praying

111

the sick, I'll cast out devils, and I'll reach out to the lost. I trust You to take all the weight of what You have established here. I'm casting all these cares upon You!

As I began to research that scripture, the weight began to lift. I discovered that the word *casting* used in that verse was the Greek word *epirrhipto*, which means to throw or hurl something violently or with great force. I went into that Sunday service rejoicing, and I truly haven't been the same since! Cares still do exist, but when we give them over to God, we don't have to carry them anymore!

Worrying about our situation will not change anything in our lives. To get to the NEXT that God has for us, we must trust Him and cast our cares onto Him. We are not designed to carry the burden of worry, fretting and anxiety. It is simply too much for the human body and the central nervous system to tolerate. The burden is too heavy for us, but it is not too heavy for Him. We can trust Him.

The storm will be over soon. That emotional battle, that financial issue, will be over soon. That sickness trying to attack our bodies is temporary. The thing that has made us miserable is only momentary. The trouble making us cry in the middle of the night can be cast upon the Lord. The pain of betrayal and deception can be cast upon the Lord.

The trial we are going through is transitioning us. The children of Israel were not trapped between the Egyptian army and the Red Sea—it only looked that way to them. God's plan was to use the event to transition them into the next phase of their journey to the Promised Land. They just didn't know it yet!

We may feel the pressure of Pharaoh's army behind us, but it is only a means to an end. We may be in a great deal of pain, but it is only a temporary test.

Psalm 30:5 reminds us: ...*Weeping may endure for a night, But joy comes in the morning.* As we worship and praise God for our victory, our NEXT is being released in the heavenlies.

The children of Israel did not find the wilderness to be a comfortable place. Even though God gave them water when they were thirsty, and food when they were hungry, the wilderness wasn't comfortable or enjoyable. He gave them just enough.

He wanted them to hate the wilderness—it was intended to be a temporary place. They were supposed to find it difficult and undesirable. After all, it was a desert: hot during the day and freezing during the night.

They were supposed to learn to trust God through their hunger and thirst. He wanted them to run toward the promise, but the problem was they became adjusted to the desert mentality. Consequently, they ate manna for forty years, until an entirely new generation of Israelites had taken the place of their fathers.

Just like the Israelites, we get comfortable with scraping by. We get tired of the fight and become satisfied with having just enough to survive. We have just enough peace to keep our sanity, but not enough to sleep soundly at night. We have just enough faith to believe we will go to heaven someday, but not enough to walk in health and healing in the here and now.

NEXT

God gave them manna from heaven, water from the rock, clothes that didn't wear out, and feet that were never swollen, but all of that was just provision for the journey. It was to sustain them until they reached the promise. They were to transition from the wilderness to the land of wonder.

We have to guard against getting stuck in the desert. Our light affliction is not even worthy to be compared to the glory that is about to be revealed to us. God has a breakthrough for us on the other side of the desert.

Being stuck in a desert mentality produces its own form of bondage—a prison that keeps us from inheriting the promises that belong to us. In a time of testing, the outcome can either go one way or the other. Looking only at our trials obscures our vision of victory; focusing on our crisis keeps us from seeing the possibility of celebrating success.

SEEING THE UNSEEN

When Paul and Silas were preaching in the city of Philippi, they were arrested for setting a young slave girl free from the demonic power that had her bound, a power that had produced a good income for her masters. They were taken before the magistrates, pronounced guilty, beaten, humiliated, and thrown into the innermost part of the dungeon. Despite all this, in the middle of their midnight hour, they begin to pray and sing praises unto God. They didn't know it yet, but their purpose in that prison was about to be revealed. At that moment, the jail began to shake until all the prisoner's doors were opened, and their chains fell off.

And the keeper of the prison, awaking from sleep and seeing the prison doors open, supposing the prisoners had fled, drew his sword and was about to kill himself. But Paul called with a loud voice, saying, "Do yourself no harm, for we are all here."

Then he called for a light, ran in, and fell down trembling before Paul and Silas. And he brought them out and said, "Sirs, what must I do to be saved?"

So they said, "Believe on the Lord Jesus Christ, and you will be saved, you and your household." Then they spoke the word of the Lord to him and to all who were in his house.

Acts 16:27-32

The jailer had never experienced anything like this before, and he was understandably shaken. But he recognized that he needed to know the God they had been worshiping. The jailer and his whole family were saved and baptized, because Paul and Silas chose to praise God in the middle of their midnight.

They didn't complain. They didn't fuss or cuss; they didn't sit silently in their situation. They prayed and praised in one accord, and all the prisoners heard them.

God does His best work in the darkest moments of our lives. When we begin to pray and praise, we can move from pain into purpose, from sickness into wellness, from darkness into light, from lost to found, from weeping to rejoicing, and from lack into divine overflow. Doors will fly open for us if we can just see the unseen.

Freedom is ours, on the other side of the Red Sea.

> **Prayer and Praise**

NEXT

The desert we find ourselves in may not even be of our own making. The new generation of Israelites who were born into the wilderness may have inherited the old circumstances, but they adopted a new mindset. For them, it was time to enter into their Promised Land, no longer held back by those who could not see the unseen. They knew there were giants in the land, but they knew their God was able. They disregarded the visible, and they observed the invisible! They were ready for their NEXT!

Victory comes when we agree with God—when we say the same thing about our situation that He says about it. If we will fill ourselves with the Word of God, we can boldly and determinedly make these declarations:

- I can't see sickness anymore because all I can see is: *By His stripes, I am healed.* (based on Isaiah 53:5)
- I can't see that financial problem any longer because all I can see is: *My God will supply all my needs according to His riches in glory by Christ Jesus.* (based on Philippians 4:19)
- I can't see myself struggling through the wilderness of "just enough" anymore because: *My God is able to do exceeding, abundantly above all that I can think, ask or imagine.* (based on Ephesians 3:20)
- I can see the things that are not seen because they are eternal. (based on 2 Corinthians 4:18)
- I can see my children saved and filled with the Holy Ghost and doing the work of God. (based on Acts 16:31)
- I can see a fresh anointing being released in my life. (based on Isaiah 43:19)

We will certainly encounter difficulties in this life, but once we catch a glimpse of the eternal, our vision will change. We will go from seeing only the *seen*, to being able to see the *unseen*.

My twin brother and I are no longer those two tiny babies, fighting for every breath. The enemy's plan to take us out has only made us stronger and brought a greater measure of glory to God than would have been possible without a fight.

Our beginning may have been dark, but the future is bright. Your present may seem dark, but God is ready to bring you out into the light! He is ready to take you into your NEXT!

When we start talking about where we are going instead of where we have been, things will change. When we start talking about what we are *expecting* instead of what we have been *experiencing*, things will change. And when those things begin to change, God will get all the glory as we step into our NEXT!